The Forward book of poetry

2015

The Forward book of poetry

2015

FORWARD
Worldwide

London

First published in Great Britain by
Forward Worldwide · 83 Clerkenwell Road · London EC1R 5AR
in association with
Faber and Faber · Bloomsbury House · 74–77 Great Russell Street
London WC1B 3DA

ISBN 978 0 571 31524 6 (paperback)

Printed and bound in the UK by CPI Group (UK) Ltd, Croydon CR0 4YY

A CIP catalogue reference for this book
is available at the British Library.

To Felix Dennis. In memoriam

Contents

Highly Commended Poems 2014

Foreword

The other day, a young reporter – a man of great ambition and some determination – asked me what I thought of his work. It was competent, but his writing was plodding. I recommended he read a poem a day. It wasn't original advice. I'd plagiarised it from my colleague Alan Little, one of the BBC's best, and most scandalously under-used, reporters.

Most striking was the young journalist's reply.

'But where would I find any poetry?' he said.

So far has poetry tumbled out of the public consciousness that a bright young man – and one who makes his living by words, no less – had no idea where he might discover it.

Does it matter? Aren't we surrounded by thousands of lyrical expressions of emotion in song every day? I think it does matter.

In a time when journalism, marketing and sloganising has sucked the life out of language – when everything is a crisis or a tragedy, when multinational corporations offer to salvage our marriages and salve our consciences not for love but for profit, when commuters delayed by leaves on the line are said to suffer 'misery', we need the precision and resonance of poetry more then ever.

Years ago (I can't quite recall how it happened) I helped to judge the English hedge-laying championships. Now, while a well-laid hedge is a delight, to appreciate the quality of the work, you need to be familiar with the different idioms of different parts of the country, the tools used, the appropriate woods.

Poetry judging is a little like that and yet the greatest poems of our history achieved their status not just because other poets thought they were pretty good, but because they also resonated with the public. Posterity is a mixed jury.

I was asked to chair the Forward Prize judges as a representative of that many-headed, semi-mythical creature the Common Reader. There is nothing common about the Common Reader, but for the purposes of this foreword, it's useful to imagine her, or him, as someone who is not a poet, but who comes to poetry to be delighted, comforted or alerted, to see the ordinary as extraordinary, the everyday as profound, to have the world reimagined, language revived. The arresting phrase, the telling metaphor, the resonant rhyme is like a first kiss: we all know what osculation is, but, by God, it's different when your own lips are involved.

The problem is not that people don't like poetry – look at the YouTube audiences for spoken word or send anyone you know a link to Benedict Cumberbatch's reading of Keats' 'Ode to a Nightingale' if you doubt me. Yet, for some reason – shyness? fear of sounding pretentious or ignorant? – contemporary poetry plays very little part in the general cultural conversation, unlike contemporary films or plays, television drama or art exhibitions. Worse, we don't talk about why we don't talk about it. When I noted a few months ago that the number of people writing poetry now exceeded the number reading, or, at any rate, buying it and that too many poets, resigned to small audiences, seem to have connived at their own irrelevance, I was deluged in disdain. How dare the village idiot hold forth on the use of the ducking stool? QED, I rather think.

Provocation aside, the three Forward Prizes and the publication of this collection – now in its 23rd edition – are missionary work. The aim is to increase the audience for contemporary poetry by giving readers a snapshot that demonstrates the immense variety of poetry being published in Britain and Ireland today. The poems that follow are long and short, intimate and wry, insightful and arresting. A couple of them made me cry and several made me smile.

I am extremely grateful to my fellow judges, the three poets Dannie Abse, Vahni Capildeo and Helen Mort and the singer-songwriter Cerys Matthews. Was it enough that poet A was trying to do new things with form when so little was being said? Why was B's skill at slipping between two languages somehow less deft and original than C's? And at what point in reading poet D's work did we stop congratulating ourselves on spotting the endless borrowings? Dannie Abse deserves special thanks for devising a voting system of such simplicity and psychological acuteness that each of us left the shortlisting stage convinced that our tastes had been fully represented.

What follows is a selection of the poems that the judges liked, all published within a single year – from October 2013 to September 2014. There's hardly one of them I don't feel better for having read, and none that I could have written myself. I hope you enjoy them.

Jeremy Paxman, *June 2014*

Preface

I FOUNDED THE FORWARD PRIZES with a simple aim: I wanted good contemporary poetry to be better known and valued more. With the prizes' prominence, the aim has grown: poetry needs to be talked about and that conversation needs to be open to all, even to those who think poetry is not for them.

But to what end? We are regularly asked to quantify the 'impact' of our work. It's a head-scratcher: poetry is no wonder drug whose efficacy can be clinically proven, nor is it a process with measurable inputs and outputs. Cows convert grass into milk. Poets cannot be milked, or herded.

They can, however, be heard. This year we asked the shortlisted writers to speak of the paths that led them to poetry. Extracts from their responses feature in the biographies on page 163 and the full interviews, published in the eBook version of this anthology, contain some striking insights.

One struck me with force. All these writers are readers. 'What the Forward does, isn't just to hand out prizes – though that encouragement and validation means a lot – it also surveys the year's work by a large number of poets through the Forward anthology,' says John Burnside, shortlisted for Best Collection. 'It is always good to know more about the company you keep.'

For Burnside, whose poetry, novels, stories and memoirs have earned him a passionate following, reading is a political act. 'It seems to me that poetry is a defence of care over the language, its richness, its subtleties, its possibilities. If we keep reading poetry and so educating ourselves in metaphor, we can see through and scoff at the deceptive myths peddled by certain politicians and salespeople, say, or the greenwashing of major corporations – and we can remind ourselves that a bad metaphor is as much a lie as a bad narrative.'

Vidyan Ravinthiran, shortlisted for the Best First Collection prize, takes a different tack. He inherited reverence for literature, learning and the English language from his Tamil parents, acquiring strong views of what a poem should be from his study of Keats and Tennyson as a schoolboy in Leeds. When a friend gave him the 2002 *Forward Book of Poetry* those views buckled: 'I remember very clearly reading a poem by

Caitriona O'Reilly and thinking *this is great but it isn't a poem*. I had these old-fashioned ideas about what a poem should be, and I couldn't square them with the excitements of free verse. Until eventually I decided, well, if this isn't poetry, it's something else exciting – so I'll try that too…'

Those two phrases – 'a defence of care over the language' and 'something else exciting' – could both be mottoes for this year's anthology. Regular Forward anthology readers will recognise names – Douglas Dunn, Sheenagh Pugh, Denise Riley – but more than half of the poems within are by new and emerging writers. Will these stand the test of time? Maybe years hence, children currently lisping their first words will, like Ravinthiran, find their eyes and ears alerted to fresh metaphors and forms of language by this book.

The Forward Arts Foundation owes a great debt to the 2014 judges and chair Jeremy Paxman, whose own language did so much this year to take the conversation about poetry to the widest possible audience. His suggestion that poets should answer questions about idiom and form would surely have escaped notice had it not been for one word – 'inquisition' – deployed with the guile of a fisherman selecting a fly. To Jeremy, and all those who rose to his bait, including commentators from America, Australia, Canada to India and Pakistan, many thanks.

The songwriter and musician Cerys Matthews and the poets Dannie Abse, Vahni Capildeo and Helen Mort each brought lifetimes immersed in poetry to the judging process. They did this with generosity and sensitivity. The artist Gary Hume, whose cover for this year's book combines delicacy, precision and blazing visual power, has added immensely to our thinking about the ways in which poetry and contemporary art can work together.

Thank you too to the Forward Worldwide team, especially Casey Jones, Will Scott, Karen Heaney, Naomi Misquita-Rice, Christopher Stocks and Peter Davies. Forward Worldwide supports us financially, but their commitment to excellence in publishing this book is beyond price.

Rebecca Blackwood and Clare Cumberlidge of ThirteenWays have transformed the ways in which we work, giving new meaning to the words 'strategic' and 'curatorial'. Maggie Fergusson, Rachel Page and all at the Royal Society of Literature gave us space and moral support. Tim Shortis and Julie Blake of Poetry by Heart are friends and advisors, as is John Field. James Runcie and Jude Kelly of Southbank Centre have enabled us to reach new audiences by co-producing our awards ceremony directed this year by a former Forward judge, the actor Samuel West. Emma Harding interviewed the judges talking about poetry and deftly edited their words into memorable podcasts. Thanks too, to our interns, Betty Ansah and Eloise Sykes.

Arts Council England, the John Ellerman Foundation and the Esmée Fairbairn Foundation all fund the work of the Forward Arts Foundation. They are joined this year by a new supporter, the Rothschild Foundation. We are grateful to them all.

This year, our longest-standing individual patron, Felix Dennis, died. He numbered poetry among his great loves alongside trees, wine, and what can loosely be described as 'living life to the full'. His favourite poems were those he wrote, but despite this bias – one many poets share – he consistently encouraged rivals through the Felix Dennis Prize for Best First Collection. He will be much missed.

Finally, thanks to our trustees, Nigel Bennett, Robyn Marsack, Martin Thomas and especially Joanna Mackle – whose support for the prizes is as long-standing as the prizes themselves – and to the Forward Arts Foundation executive team, Susannah Herbert and Maisie Lawrence.

William Sieghart, *June 2014*

Shortlisted Poems
The Forward Prize for Best Collection

Colette Bryce

Derry

I was born between the Creggan and the Bogside
    to the sounds of crowds and smashing glass,
by the river Foyle with its suicides and rip tides.
    I thought that city was nothing less

than the whole and rain-domed universe.
    A teacher's daughter, I was one of nine
faces afloat in the looking-glass
    fixed in the hall, but which was mine?

I wasn't ever sure.
    We walked to school, linked hand in hand
in twos and threes like paper dolls.
    I slowly grew to understand

the way the grey Cathedral cast
    its shadow on our learning, cool,
as sunlight crept from east to west.
    The adult world had tumbled into hell

from where it wouldn't find its way
    for thirty years. The local priest
played Elvis tunes and made us pray
    for starving children, and for peace,

and lastly for 'The King'. At mass we'd chant
    hypnotically, *Hail Holy Queen,*
mother of mercy; sing to Saint
    Columba of his *Small oak grove, O Derry mine.*

*

We'd cross the border in our red Cortina,
    stopped at the checkpoint just too long
for fractious children, searched by a teenager
    drowned in a uniform, cumbered with a gun,

who seemed to think we were trouble-on-the-run
    and not the Von Trapp Family Singers
harmonizing every song
    in rounds to pass the journey quicker.

Smoke coiled up from terraces
    and fog meandered softly down the valley
to the Brandywell and the greyhound races,
    the ancient walls with their huge graffiti,

arms that encircled the old city
    solidly. Beyond their pale,
the Rossville flats – mad vision of modernity;
    snarling crossbreeds leashed to rails.

A robot under remote control like us
    commenced its slow acceleration
towards a device at number six,
    home of the moderate politician;

only a hoax, for once, some boys
    had made from parcel tape and batteries
gathered on forays to the BSR,
    the disused electronics factory.

*

The year was nineteen eighty-one,
    the reign of Thatcher. 'Under Pressure'
was the song that played from pub to pub
    where talk was all of hunger strikers

in the Maze, our jail within a jail.
    A billboard near Free Derry Corner
clocked the days to the funerals
    as riots blazed in the city centre.

Each day, we left for the grammar school,
    behaved ourselves, pulled up our socks
for benevolent Sister Emmanuel
    and the Order of Mercy. Then we'd flock

to the fleet of buses that ferried us
    back to our lives, the Guildhall Square
where Shena Burns our scapegoat drunk
    swayed in her chains like a dancing bear.

On the couch, we cheered as an Irish man
    bid for the Worldwide Featherweight title
and I saw blue bruises on my mother's arms
    when her sleeve fell back while filling the kettle

for tea. My bed against the door,
    I pushed the music up as loud
as it would go and curled up on the floor
    to shut the angry voices out.

*

My candle flame faltered in a cup;
    we were stood outside the barracks in a line
chanting in rhythm, calling for a stop
    to strip searches for the Armagh women.

The proof that Jesus was a Derry man?
    Thirty-three, unemployed and living with his mother,
the old joke ran. While half the town
    were queuing at the broo, the fortunate others

bent to the task of typing out the cheques.
    Boom! We'd jump at another explosion,
windows buckling in their frames, and next
    you could view the smouldering omission

in a row of shops, the missing tooth
    in a street. Gerry Adams' mouth
was out of sync in the goldfish bowl
    of the TV screen, our dubious link

with the world. Each summer, one by one,
    my sisters upped and crossed the water,
armed with a grant from the government
    – the Butler system's final flowers –

until my own turn came about:
    I watched that place grow small before
the plane ascended through the cloud
    and I could not see it clearly any more.

A Clan Gathering

Dublin, 2009

Not a birthday only
but a clan gathering for Bríd.
Her poor old peerless eyes.
The young, peripheral.
The host, with his long jaw
and recreational shirt
distributing flutes of gold wine
to the old, the late, the rheumy-eyed,

who fill the bright reception room
with its view of the pool
and, further, the ocean; mingle,
awkward and sociable, polite
enquirers after each other's
links – a slight anxiety
to be leaves on the twigs of a
branch of the scheme of things.

They gather around
the family chart, unscrolled
on the sideboard, busily plot
themselves and theirs,
point and jostle, narratives
tumbling out of their mouths,
excitable flow of births,
deaths, accidents, marriages,

properties lost. What
it is all about, it seems,
is the simple multiplication
of the tribe. The ancients
lower themselves into chairs.
A ribboned child, somebody's

from England, picks out
phrases on the baby grand.

Bríd floats blindly through the guests,
immaculate in suit and shades.
She folds the hand of each in hers,
intent, intensely feeling her way,
heels clacking on the oak floor.
The hosts are oddly embarrassed
by their wealth, all modesty
and disconnect. In sepia,

the family heroes. Uncle Joe,
third from the left at the first Dáil,
his handsome face pure intellect…
A hand on an arm, smiles, guffaws,
a palpable text now almost visible
in the air; a set text, thick as a
swarm around the head-to-heads
and the have-you-met-yets.

I don't mention my lover,
how we have to invent
for ourselves a blank, unscripted
future; her guaranteed absence
from the diagram, the great
genetic military-campaign,
and no one asks,
sensing a difference.

Outdoors, they spill onto several
levels, settle in groups and lean
on rails as if on the various decks
of a ship. United they stand
against death and difference:
my mother, who drew nine babies
from her body, as though
from out of a conjurer's cloak;

the low-key waiters, musicians,
caterers; toddlers chasing each other
through the legs; the North-
South divide, the Celtic Tiger,
unmet cousins, country farmers.
Time for a speech from the birthday girl!
A believer, she says, in genes,
genetic inheritance.

The sea's incredible equilibrium.
Imagine a tilt and the consequence.

The cypresses.

The four-by-fours in the drive.

John Burnside

A Rival

Sometimes, when I watch you through the glass,
fixing your make-up, or twisting your hair in a plait,
I catch a passing glimpse of someone new,
someone I might have loved had we ever met
and, now that we've come this far, I must admit
that, given the choice, I'd rather her than you:
this inward self a camera might steal,
the soul that shatters when a mirror breaks
and, so they say, takes seven years to heal.
Sometimes I think if she and I were free,
she'd tell me secrets you could never share;
though, now I come to think of it, I swear
I've caught her giving you such private looks
as lovers do, when no one else can see
and then I've turned away, for all our sakes,
because it's clear she'd rather you than me.

On the Vanishing of My Sister, Aged 3, 1965

They saw her last in our garden of stones and willows.
A few bright twigs and pebbles glazed with rain
and, here and there, amidst the dirt and gravel,
a slick of leaf and milkstone, beautiful
for one long moment in the changing light.
Then she was gone.
My mother had looked away
for a matter of seconds
– she said this, over and over,
as if its logic could undo
the wildness of a universe that stayed
predictable for years, then carried off
a youngest daughter;
my father was in the room at the back of our prefab,
watching the new TV, the announcer
excited, Gold Cup Day
and Arkle romping home by twenty lengths.
Maybe we have to look back, to see
that we have all the makings of bliss – the first spring light,
the trees along the farm road
thick with song;
and surely it was this
that drew her out
to walk into the big
wide world, astonished, suddenly at home
no matter where she was.
It seems, when they found her,
she wasn't the least bit scared.
An hour passed, then another;
my mother waited, while our friends and neighbours
came and went, my father running out
to search, then back again,
taking her, once, in his arms, and trying
vainly to reassure her,
she in her apron,

dusted with icing and flour,
and he too self-contained, too rudely male,
more awkward, now, than when he knew her first:
a marriage come between them, all those years
of good intent
and blithe misunderstanding.
It was Tom Dow who brought her home,
tears in his eyes, the boy we had always known
as the local bully, suddenly finding himself
heroic,
and when they brought her in
and sat her down,
we gathered to stand
in the light of her, life and death
inscribed in the blue of her eyes, and the sweet
confusion of rescue, never having been
endangered.
She's married now, and Tom is married too,
and I, like my father, strayed into
discontent,
not being what was wanted, strange to myself
and wishing, all the time,
that I was lost,
out at the end of winter, turning away
to where the dark begins, far in the trees,
darkness and recent cold and the sense of another
far in the trees, where no one pretends
I belong.

Louise Glück

An Adventure

1.

It came to me one night as I was falling asleep
that I had finished with those amorous adventures
to which I had long been a slave. Finished with love?
my heart murmured. To which I responded that many profound
discoveries
awaited us, hoping, at the same time, I would not be asked
to name them. For I could not name them. But the belief that they
existed –
surely this counted for something?

2.

The next night brought the same thought,
this time concerning poetry, and in the nights that followed
various other passions and sensations were, in the same way,
set aside forever, and each night my heart
protested its future, like a small child being deprived of a favorite toy.
But these farewells, I said, are the way of things.
And once more I alluded to the vast territory
opening to us with each valediction. And with that phrase I became
a glorious knight riding into the setting sun, and my heart
became the steed underneath me.

3.

I was, you will understand, entering the kingdom of death,
though why this landscape was so conventional
I could not say. Here, too, the days were very long
while the years were very short. The sun sank over the far mountain.
The stars shone, the moon waxed and waned. Soon
faces from the past appeared to me:
my mother and father, my infant sister; they had not, it seemed,
finished what they had to say, though now
I could hear them because my heart was still.

4.
At this point, I attained the precipice
but the trail did not, I saw, descend on the other side;
rather, having flattened out, it continued at this altitude
as far as the eye could see, though gradually
the mountain that supported it completely dissolved
so that I found myself riding steadily through the air –
All around, the dead were cheering me on, the joy of finding them
obliterated by the task of responding to them –

5.
As we had all been flesh together,
now we were mist.
As we had been before objects with shadows,
now we were substance without form, like evaporated chemicals.
Neigh, neigh, said my heart,
or perhaps nay, nay – it was hard to know.

6.
Here the vision ended. I was in my bed, the morning sun
contentedly rising, the feather comforter
mounded in white drifts over my lower body.
You had been with me –
there was a dent in the second pillow case.
We had escaped from death –
or was this the view from the precipice?

The Horse and Rider

Once there was a horse, and on the horse there was a rider. How handsome they looked in the autumn sunlight, approaching a strange city! People thronged the streets or called from the high windows. Old women sat among flower pots. But when you looked about for another horse or another rider, you looked in vain. My friend, said the animal, why not abandon me? Alone, you can find your way here. But to abandon you, said the other, would be to leave a part of myself behind, and how can I do that when I do not know which part you are?

Kei Miller

Establishing the Metre

Like tailors who must know their clients' girths
two men set out to find the sprawling measure of the earth.
They walked the curve from Rodez to Barcelona,
and Barcelona to Dunkirk. Such a pilgrimage!
They did not call it inches, miles or chains –
this distance which as yet had no clear name.
Between France and Spain they dared to stretch
uncalibrated measuring tapes. And foot
by weary foot, they found a rhythm
the measure that exists in everything.

In Which the Cartographer Asks for Directions

Sometimes the cartographer gets frustrated when he asks an I-formant how to get to such and such a place, and the I-formant might say something like –

> Awrite, you know the big white house at the bottom of
> Clover Hill with all the windows dem board up, and
> with a high shingle roof that look almost like a church?

Yes, the cartographer says.

> And in front the house you always see a ole woman,
> only three teeth in her mouth, and she out there selling
> pepper shrimp in a school chair with a umbrella tie to it.
> And beside her she always have two mongrel dog and
> one of them is white and the nedda one is brown?

Yes, I know exactly where you mean, the cartographer says.

> And in the yard there is a big guinnep tree that hang
> right out to the road, so school pickney always stop
> there to buy shrimp and eat free guinnep?

Yes, yes, the cartographer insists. I know it.

> Good, says the I-formant. Cause you mustn' go there.

Hugo Williams

Love Poem

I suppose you're right and breaking up
would be quite a good thing,
but staying together
would be an equally good thing,
so whatever we decide to do
it will be all right. On balance,
I lean towards doing nothing,
but whatever happens we'll go on
seeing each other, won't we?

I suppose it wouldn't be so bad,
seeing other people for a change,
we might even find someone
we could bear to be with
for more than half an hour,
although I doubt it somehow.
Experience suggests we go on
feeling the same about everything
no matter what happens. I do anyway.

I Knew the Bride

for my sister Polly 1950–2004

You had to go to bed ahead of us
even then, while your two older brothers
grabbed another hour downstairs.
The seven-year gap
was like a generation between us.
You played the princess,
swanning about the house
in your tablecloth wedding dress,
till we told you your knickers were dirty
and you ran upstairs to change.
Your hair was tied up
in plaits on top of your head,
showing the parting down the back
as you marched out of the room.

It wouldn't be long
till we were asking you to dance,
practising our jiving
for the Feather's Club Ball at the Lyceum.
Nobody knew so well
how to judge the turns
with perfectly tensed arms,
your ponytail flying back and forth
to 'Party Doll' by Buddy Knox.
For my speech on your wedding day
all I had to do
was read out the words
to Nick Lowe's 'I Knew the Bride
When She Used to Rock 'n' Roll'.

You used to do the pony,
you used to do the stroll,
but the bride in her wedding dress
spinning round on top of the cake,
wound down to a sense of loss
when your coach didn't come
and questions of identity
rained on your party.
The bride turned out
to be less a princess
than a walk-on part
as a lady-in-waiting
in a film of Cinderella,
The Slipper and the Rose.

A life of go-sees and
castings, followed by
the odd screen test, gave way
to a different sort of test,
with shadows for faces.
When you first crossed over
into that wintry place
you said you had a feeling even then.
The different parts of you
turned against one another,
as if they could hear you thinking.
'What you don't realise', you said,
in your new winter bonnet,
'is that hair goes with everything.'

You put yourself together
for occasional family lunches
at the Brompton Brasserie,
appearing coiffed and chic
and on time, so that I imagined you
going about all day looking like that
and even assumed you were getting better.
You fought a five-year war
with that foul thing
which deals in hope and fear,
two against one,
like the two brothers who tormented you.
It wouldn't be long
till you had to go to bed.

You turned your back on us
to protect us from your face.
You lay on the rack of yourself,
murdered by your skeleton.
Somewhere towards the end
you climbed its rickety ladder
to your full height
and stood before us one last time.
You had ordered a white stetson
from a Country music catalogue.
Perched on your coffin, it sailed
ahead of you into the flames.
I saw the parting down the back of your head
as you marched out of the room.

Shortlisted Poems
The Felix Dennis Prize for
Best First Collection

Fiona Benson

Devonport

Holstered in the Tamar
the low-slung bolts
of submarines come home.

Each breached hood
looks like part of the wharf –
black pontoon or tidal berth

and breathes no word
of its underwater heft,
its airlocks and vaults,

its sintered, nuclear core.
Pray for our fathers on leave
who, in the unstable crucibles

of sleep, crawl
through drowning rooms
of war and sorrow.

Pray for the difficult undoing
of each shining, fissioned load,
the slow decay of isotopes.

Would that the old wars were done with.
The sea is still a torpedo-path,
an Armageddon road.

Breastfeeding

i

But really it's like this –
weeping as your milk comes in,
clutching a hot poultice
and counting through the pain
as you bring her on
to the hardened breast.

There's a whole new grammar
of tongue-tie and latch –
the watery foremilk
with its high acid content,
the fatty hindmilk
that separates in the fridge

to a thick skim
at the top of the flask,
and the nursing bra
like a complex lock
as you fumble, one-handed
at the catch.

ii

She has a stomach
the size of a marble
and feeds in and out
of days.

You are lost
to the manifold
stations of milk,
the breast siphoned off

then filling,
yellow curd
of the baby's shit
you get down on your knees

at the foot of the change-mat
to clean,
holding your breath.
It was always like this;

a long line of women
sitting and kneeling,
out of their skins
with love and exhaustion.

Liz Berry

Nailmaking

Nailing was wenches' werk.
Give a girl of eight an anvil and a little ommer
and by God er'd swing it,
batter the glowing iron into tidy spikes
ready fer hoofing some great sod oss
who'd lost its shoe in the muck.

The nimble ones was best,
grew sharp and quick as the nails they struck
from the scorching fire.
Eighteen, er could turn out two hundred an hour,
tongue skimming the soot on er lips,
onds moulding heat.

In the small brick nailshop
four of 'em werked wi' faces glistening
in the hot smoke. Fust the point was forged
then the rod sunk deep into the bore
so the head could be punched –
round fer regulars, diamond fer frost nails.

Marry a nailing fella and yo'll be a pit oss
fer life, er sisters had told er,
but er'd gone to him anyway in er last white frock
and found a new black ommer
waiting fer er in 'is nailshop
under a tablecloth veil.

ommer hammer; *er* her, she; *oss* horse

Black Country

Commuters saw it first, vast
on the hillside by the A41,
a wingless Pegasus, hooves
kicking road into the distance.

It had appeared over night.
A black shadow on the scrub,
galloping above the gates
of the derelict factories,

facing East, towards the pits,
mouth parted as if it would
swallow the sun that rose
from behind the winding gear.

Word spread. Crowds gathered.
Kids, someone said,
but when they examined its flanks
they found pure coal,

coal where none had been mined
in years, where houses
still collapsed into empty shafts
and hills bore scars.

A gift from the underworld,
hauling the past
from the dead earth. Old men
knelt to breathe the smoke

of its mane, whisper
in its ear, walked away
in silence, fists clenched,
faces streaked with tears.

Niall Campbell

‘The Letter Always Arrives at its Destination’

– then I wrote often to the sea,
to its sunk rope and its salt bed,
to the large weed mass lipping the bay.

The small glass bottles would be lined
along the bedroom floor – ship green
or church-glass clear – such envelopes

of sea-mail. Only on the day
of sending would a note be fed
into each swollen, brittle hull –

I had my phases: for so long
it was maps: maps of wader nests,
burrows and foxes dens, maps where

nothing was in its true position –
my landscape blooming from the surf.
Later, I’d write my crushes’ names

onto the paper, as a small gift.
The caps then tested and wax sealed.
None ever reached my dreamed America,

its milk-white shore, as most would sink
between the pier and the breakwater,
and I would find that I had written

about the grass to the drowned sand,
again; and to the sunken dark,
I had sent all the light I knew.

Harvest

I've been thinking too much about the night
I slipped and the coal scattered on the snowed drive.

Then it was time spent in luck's appleyard
gathering its black fruit; or it was time

collecting what I'd left too long to gather,
a harvest all wilt and harrowed – anyway,

it was time spent, and I held the steel bucket,
filled it to the sound of nothing at all.

Beatrice Garland

Beach Holiday

You are sitting eating an orange,
not giving me any
and staring straight out to sea.

The sand in front of me
is pocked with little craters,
every one a wild salt tear.

Why did we come to Spain
to have this row?
We could have stayed at home and watch it rain.

You say you'll forgive me
if I understand what it is
you're forgiving me for.

I am in a difficult position.
I want this to be over
so the beach can go back to normal

and all the figures jump about and bat
their brightly coloured beach balls
in golden light once more

but I cannot ask you to remind me
of what it was I did (or said) so
I say nothing.

Why do you think it's called
making love anyway, idiot?
You stride off into the ocean

and are gone a long time.
I watch its foamy edges smooth the sand
and change my mind. I want you to be alive.

Indissoluble, how well we know each other.
These ructions, mutinies, aren't they just
protests at the gravity of love?

Hating to know how deep it goes,
that need for one who finds you in a crowd,
who comes back home at night and stays and stays.

Lady and Fox

You, dog fox, dancer in the dark,
snapper-up of unconsidered trifles,
don't look at me like that.

You're curling your lip at me, moon-hunter,
backing away needle-toothed,
winged ears flattening against the bone.

Stop fretting about those sleeping pigeons
and hold my gaze. You're a handsome beast
for a city dweller: could turn a lady into fox.

I want to grab you, mouse-catcher,
in your marvellously-tailored dream-coat,
dig my fingers into your furred lapels

and hold on tight for a rough ride.
And we could join forces, bone-cruncher:
I'd cook up those chickens for the two of us.

So show me the foxtrot, rats' bane,
and I'll teach you the slow waltz.
Before you disappear into the dark

let's go out on the razzle –
you in your carnival mask,
me in my red fox fur.

Kevin Powers

Great Plain

Here is where appreciation starts, the boy
in a dusty velour tracksuit almost getting shot.
When I say boy, I mean it. When I say almost
getting shot, I mean exactly that. For bringing
unexploded mortars right up to us
takes a special kind of courage I don't have.
A dollar for each one, I'm told,
on orders from brigade HQ
to let the children do the dirty work.

When I say, I'd say fuck that, let the bastards find them
with the heels of boots and who cares if I mean us
as bastards and who cares if heels of boots mean things
that once were, the way grass once was a green thing
and now is not, the way the muezzin call once was
five times today and now is not

and when I say heel of boot I hope you'll appreciate
that I really mean the gone foot, any one of us

timbered and inert and when I say green
I mean like fucking Nebraska, wagon wheels on the prairie
and other things that can't be appreciated
until you're really far away and they come up
as points of reference.

I don't know what Nebraska looks like.
I've never been. When I say Nebraska
I mean the idea of, the way an ex-girlfriend of mine
once talked about the idea of a gun. But guns are not ideas.
They are not things to which comparisons are made. They are

one weight in my hand when the little boy crests the green hill
and the possibilities of shooting him or not extend out from me
like the spokes of a wheel. The hills are not green anymore
and in my mind they never were, though when I say they were
I mean I'm talking about reality. I appreciate that too,

knowing
the hills were green,
knowing
someone else has paid him
for his scavenging, one less

exploding thing beneath our feet.
I appreciate the fact
that for at least one day I don't have to decide
between dying and shooting a little boy.

Blue Star Mother

Compare my sins to this, for instance,
my mother refusing to have her picture taken,
always raising up her hands the moment that
the shutter clicks, so that looking back
on the photographic
evidence of my life
one could be easily convinced
I was raised by a woman
whose face was the palm of a hand.

This is not the case. I know that
in the seventies she wore
large glasses, apparently sat often enough
on cheap imitation teak couches
to be photographed on them more than once, sometimes
had her hair done up
in whatever fashion
wives of factory workers
wore in Richmond
and was beautiful.

But after hanging her blue star up she covered it
with curtains. She stopped
going to the hairdresser
and took up gardening instead.
Which is to say, that when she woke up
in the middle of the night
she'd stand in the yard in her nightgown
staring at a clump of dead azaleas
running down beside the house.
Later, she stopped sleeping.
Later still, her hair went grey.

I had a picture of her
in my helmet, shuffled in
with other pictures.
I think it was in between
some cut out from
a *Maxim* magazine and
a Polaroid of my girlfriend's tits
with a note on it that said,
Sorry, last one, be safe, XOXO.

My mother told me
about a dream she had
before the sleeping stopped. I died
and woke her at her bedside
to tell her I was dead,
though I would not have
had to tell her because
I'd already bled on her favorite floral rug
and half my jaw was missing.
I don't know what to make of that.

I like to think she caught
some other mother's dream,
because she could take
how hard the waiting was,
and had all that practice
getting up her hands.

Vidyan Ravinthiran

Snow

What I'm saying is, this isn't the right kind of snow.
Sure the anchors call it treacherous
but I've met it down dark alleys all my life. No,
snow should always be, as kids have it, a miracle
of whiteness at the pane, flakes large enough
to plink at the glass like a moth or a fingernail

and dry out slow enough to watch drying out
on the clothing of the one you love. Forget
the ice-box favoured in the emergency room,
it's snow like this a heart comes bedded in.
And forget those now useless runways;
planes in mid-air grow sensitive,

the riveted metal of their wings goosepimples
as they go swooping through two kinds of white.
The difference between snow and water is
the difference between dialectic and a kiss,
between a birth certificate and spare change.
This much you already know. What you don't know

is snow, is slanted crystals
the halo round a sodium lamp
can't bear without shuddering.
While credit shifts and melts and hardens
and is lost, as the great man says,
as *water is in water*, his words are merely

so many thought-bubbles made visible
as we breathe in a snowy climate:
white shapes of breath that want, like the smoke
from a cigarette, or the super-slow-mo ripples
of a cube of gelatine bounced off tile, to be
the drapes and folds of statuary. The bare

ruined choir, the coloured glass is stained
to a white radiance and goes
without remainder into water, a new beginning;
yet the snow we ball and build
into forts we'll live in when all grown up
wants to change, always, into a white beard.

A Chair Addresses Jackie Chan

As you somersault into my seat and spin
my legs in a henchman's face, I know
I love you, always have... Though one
might consider ours an abusive relationship.
Your own bruises, do they remember
how I held you, moved just as you desired
– or am I simply more of the scenery
bullets chewed to make that crucial
inch between my splintering flesh
and yours enthralling as the Gaza Strip
played for laughs? You are the realist
and I am a piece of your code, the mundane
detail which makes this room appear
an actual room in which to live and fight
to keep well-wrought urns from tottering
off their improbably thin pedestals,
holding before your face the explosive vest
so the gun-toting tough is comically arrested.
Yet I know my worth. I know you
have nightmares, of empty rooms, with no
urns or kitchen sinks or silly little chairs
to work with. There, your kung-fu bricolage
shrivels to nothing like the limbs of a saint.

Shortlisted Poems
The Forward Prize for Best Single Poem

Tim Nolan

Red Wing Correctional Facility

Along the bluffs, the limestone Main Building
has the manner of 19th century discipline
and retribution for somewhat small juvenile
wrongs. The wrongs are greater now, I'm thinking,
as I get buzzed in, escorted through several doors,
and taken in an unmarked car about half a block
to the room of boys, black boys, laughing and strutting,
and I'm there to talk about poetry and life, so I start
with Walt Whitman, to blow out the pipes because
you want to blow the dust out of that old church music
to find one's own song and Walt is the best, and the boys
are listening, each of them listening, from Chicago
and New Orleans and Minneapolis, listening as I read
"Crossing Brooklyn Ferry" and they are right there with Walt
right there with his voice which they already know somehow
and I suggest what poetry can do, that it can cross mountains
escape prisons (they laugh like *yeah sure*) that words
can go to the stars and back and by breathing Shakespeare's sonnet
you can inhabit Shakespeare's very vocal chords. So,
we're going along like this and I mention *The Soul* not in some
religious sense but in the sense that each of us has a *Soul*, that sense
we get in a moment that there is something magnificent in us
that is not us but somehow is and the boys are listening very
closely to my words from each of their places around the table –
Omar, Ken, Josh, Jordan, James – and I get them in the mood
to write and they start writing, some in small precise script,
some in blocky letters, some in flourishes that end
with a celebrity signature and now I have them read
their favorite poem of the poems they've just written and now
they read their second-favorite poem until they've read everything
they've written today and I say *Big voices, men, let's have these
big slow voices* and they get courage in their words each one
of the words they picked and I ask them to write a poem called

Red Wing and they moan a poem called *Red Wing* which is
the *facility* within which they are to be *corrected* and I have them
begin with *The River*, then *The Trees*, then *The Stars*
and they say unremarkable things about the river and the trees,
and the stars they never see because it's always too late for stars
or too early and the lights, the lights are always too bright.

Denise Riley

AFTER LA ROCHEFOUCAULD

'It is more shameful to distrust your friends
Than be deceived by them': things in themselves
Do hold – a pot, a jug, a jar, Sweet Williams'
Greenshank shins – so that your eye's pulled
Clear of metallic thought by the light constancy
Of things, that rest there with you. Or without.
That gaily deadpan candour draws you on –
Your will to hope rises across their muteness.

Stephen Santus

In a Restaurant

This gesture I make to ask for the bill,
Writing on the air
With an imaginary ballpoint,
I learnt from Christopher,
Who learnt it from his father,
Who learnt it himself somewhere.

Christopher's father is long dead:
He echoes less and less.
How strange that what survives of us
Is what we would hardly guess.

Jack Underwood

'Thank You for Your Email'

Two years ago I was walking up a mountain path
having been told of excellent views from the summit.
The day was clear and hot, the sky wide and cloudless.
There was only the sound of my breath, my boots treading,
and the faint clonking of cowbells back down the track.
What little wind there was on the climb soon dropped
as I reached the summit, as if it had been distracted
or called upon to cover events elsewhere. I drank eagerly,
catching my breath, and then took in the view, which was
as spectacular as I had been told. I could make out a tree,
a shrub, really (it being so distant in the valley below
I couldn't say how high), silently on fire, the smoke
trailing a vertical black line before dissipating. I watched
the flames consume the whole shrub. No one came to stop it.
No one seemed to be around to see it, and I felt very alone.
From nowhere a great tearing came: a fighter-jet, low
and aggressive, ripped above me and, surprised, I dropped
on one knee and watched it zoom, bellowing overhead.
As it passed I saw a shred of something fall, a rag, spinning.
I shielded my eyes to see, bewildered and pinned watching
the object, the rag, gather its falling weight, its speed, until
it flumped down without a bounce, only ten footsteps
to my right. It was part of a white bird, a gull. No head,
just a wing and a hunk of body. No leg, or tail, just
the wing and the torso: purple and bloodied. A violent
puddle surrounded it, already mixing with the grit.
Ferrous blood wafted and I recoiled feeling suddenly
cold and very high up and the view swam madly: I saw
for a second the flaming tree as I staggered backwards
and became aware that I was sitting, I had fallen, but I felt
as if I was falling and falling still, my mind unable to
connect the events which were real and terrifying because
they were real, only now I think it was not, perhaps,

a mountain, it was not, perhaps, a shrub on fire, and not
a fighter-jet boring its noise through the sky, and I am
certain now, it was not me, or a wing or body of a broken
bird, but the fearful and forgotten things I've lied to myself
about, and to my friends, and to my family.

Jeffrey Wainwright

An Empty Street

After Ottone Rosai, *Via San Leonardo*

What is there to an empty street?
And one so commonplace,
narrow, with two high walls,
bending out of view.
No one in sight
and no one expected.
No Dame Trot for sure,
with her basket over her arm,
the check cloth covering dainties,
her hat perched so,
her pince-nez expectant.
Even she has hurried away.

***

What is there to an empty street?
The photo (bottom right,
curated later)
shows the doorway
to have been your studio
(there's a plaque).
Still no one to see.
Have they tip-toed round
another way, anxious
to preserve its vacancy for you
and leave your lines,
so carefully set forth, intact?

***

What is there to an empty street?
Let's get impatient,
let's add a sound track
somewhere beyond
but coming on this way.
We'll have a marching band,
cornets, clarinet
and big bass drum,
at least the air is moving!
Until we lose control –
the band has wheeled away.
You, or the street, has won again.

***

What is there to an empty street?
Have you seized it
for your melancholy,
shushed and deterred
all would-be passers-by,
your neighbours,
even understanding friends,
emptied them out
like plums from a paper bag
and then folded
and re-creased it
as you have it now?

***

What is there to an empty street
that you will not let it go?
There is no blood,
robbery or impiety
open to the view,
no spectacles required
to see what can be seen,

the clearly pure,
the assent to less.
You must have seen it going
before your very eyes,
but you painted on.

***

What is there to an empty street
and yet how easily
I find myself enticed
along your unfathomed carriageway.
And isn't this
what you made it for?
You paint no footfall
but I can hear my steps
and the rustle of my clothes
as I proceed along,
sidling sometimes to pass through
the viewless crowd.

***

What is there to an empty street?
With this one there is the future
possibly, which is always
curving out of sight,
naturally. Out of sight.
But no one wants to see it,
which is why you are alone
and invisible, save for what you see,
what you can't help but see:
the thickening light,
and whoever has gone before
and had to leave you here.

***

What is there to an empty street?
The bruise of the dark corner
as it fades,
the antiquity
of your painstaking lines,
verticals and horizontals,
such composure –
Nice, but how I'd love to drive
a barrel hoop
down your street,
ruddy and exulting,
a boy of nine again.

***

What is there to an empty street?
Well, look hard enough,
tap tap at it,
wait by the gate,
peer at the tree,
meditate upon the bend,
walk the footpath
back and forth
and patience
will recognise your diligence.
And as the street dissolves
you shall be beckoned.

***

What is there to an empty street?
Do not break your nails
striving to climb the wall,
do not beat upon the gate
and you will flounder
if you try to pass the bend.
Pinch yourself:

this is where you are,
plump and slow.
There is no casement,
enchanted cleft or chasm.
Nowhere to pass or tumble to.

***

What is there to an empty street?
Might it as well be
dead nature,
like a glass of juice,
a cherry and its shadow,
sometimes a cruet?
Dead nature
with its auspices,
even the tree is
motionless and dumb.
Look how stock still
you will come to be.

***

What is there to an empty street?
But I am drawn to it,
indeed I fall upon it,
it saves me
from looking elsewhere,
saves me from knowledge.
Yes, it will do,
it is as much as I can deal with.
No pundits here,
no hucksters
touting
the difficult future.

***

What is there to an empty street,
as empty as an afternoon,
paused in summer?
Only you are awake
to look at it,
always vigilant,
like the master
standing above his pupil.
Is this it?
Just as you want it?
But that cooking smell,
how long can you bear it?

***

What is there to an empty street?
The relief from indoors,
from what is behind the white gate,
inside the dull windows:
three men in hats
cheating each other at cards;
another solemn *concertino*;
a man on his haunches
with his face in his hands,
others whispering.
It is not free out here,
or genial, only quiet.

***

What is there to an empty street?
Suddenly I notice a lilac tree
spilling over the wall
just in sight, before the bend.
Or it could be plums
so prolific they colour out
the leaves.

How did I not register
so much activity,
the purpling underneath the window,
the purpling sunset
of the waiting storm?

Highly Commended Poems

Mir Mahfuz Ali

Hurricane

A storm roared over the Bay of Bengal,
a glass bull charging with its horns.
It pounded throughout the long night
as we children huddled together

inside our fatherless bungalow.
We watched our tin roof rip off.
First from its tie beams
then the ceiling joists. One by one

the rest of the house vanished
as we covered our heads with our hands
and saw our possessions take flight -
The *Koran*, *War and Peace*, *Gitanjali*,

the clothes in the alna, shoes and sandals,
sisters' dolls and brothers' cricket bats.
We children couldn't understand
what sins we'd committed,

but we asked God's forgiveness.
We thought the worst was over.
Then came the giant waves
one after the other snatching us

from the arms of our mother,
tossing us like cheap wood.
Trees fell, exposing their great roots.
Cats and cattle lay dead on the ground.

Our bodies shrivelled with water,
shuddered like old engines.
Teeth rattled to the point of rapture.
The sun came very late that day,

found us trapped in a wind-sheared tree.
We couldn't hear the birds singing
or the muezzin calling for prayer. Silence,
the new disease, swept across our land.

Midnight, Dhaka, 25 March 1971

I am a hardened camera clicking at midnight.
I have caught it all – the screeching tanks
pounding the city under the massy heat,
searchlights dicing the streets like bayonets.
Kalashnikovs mowing down rickshaw pullers,
vendor sellers, beggars on the pavements.
I click on, despite the dry and bitter dust
scratched on the lake-black water of my Nikon eye,
at a Bedford truck waiting by the roadside,
at two soldiers holding the dead by their hands and legs,
throwing them into the back, hurling
them one upon another until the floor
is loaded to the sky's armpits. The corpses stare
at our star's succulent whiteness
with their arms flung out as if to bridge a nation.
Their bodies shake when the lorry chugs.
I click as the soldiers laugh at the billboard on the bulkhead:
GUINNESS IS GOOD FOR YOU
SIX MILLION DRUNK EVERY DAY.

Eavan Boland

The Long Evenings of Their Leavetakings

My mother was married by the water.
She wore a grey coat and a winter rose.

She said her vows beside a cold seam of the Irish coast.

She said her vows near the shore where
the emigrants set down their consonantal n:

on afternoo*n*, on the e*n*d of everything, at the start of *ever*.

Yellow vestments took in light
A chalice hid underneath its veil.

Her hands were full of calla and cold weather lilies.

The mail packet dropped anchor.
A black headed gull swerved across the harbor.

Icy promises rose beside a cross-hatch of ocean and horizon.

I am waiting for the words of the service. I am waiting for
keep thee only and *all my earthly*.

All I hear is an afternoon's worth of *never*.

Daniel Boon

Crescendo

Texel hears the distant
crack of an iron-brittle
cumulonimbus incus.

Amersfoort catches the lash of a wave
as it strikes against a dijk; a whale's
fluke thumping the black-blue of the sea.

A white-knuckled fist of air is gust-punched
through *Haarlem's* straten, knocking shop doors shut,
jangling windowpanes like a zak of guilders.

Thunder claps crash through the fair in *Den Haag* and shards of glas
rend open the lucht and pan-tiles smash into vuur-dust and a child's
pinwheel
sails into a gracht as visitors from *Delft* turn towards de klank of the
Devil climbing out of the Earth.

Penny Boxall

What You Mean to Me

You say your postcode slowly for the form,
an assertion of home and where you'll return.

I get the first half, then wait on you
like the bingo-caller, intent on a full house.

"I lived in Hill Street," I say, and we gawp
at each other, both of us miles away. "So do I!"

I meet your wife: we don't need names. We name
our numbers, like convicts. Mine had a red door

and a weed-matted garden. It is the same
now, you say, and we smile like old

fishermen, dragging it all back.
We hope for more coincidence

(my father once signed a cheque
for a man in a shop who said,

"But that's *my* name," like Dad
was somehow wearing it to a party,

stealing his best lines,
making his girlfriend laugh)

(and speaking of parties, my mother met
a woman at New Year who'd Christmassed

in the house we'd barely left,
with our carpets, our just-gone past)

but we don't know where to start.
You fumble with your wallet.

"What's your pin-number?" I want to ask,
in case we match again. For a year, innocent,

we'd shaped our no-shape lives
between the skimmed-milk walls, just feet

apart. *Who are you?* Please, identify.
Can you tell me what you know of me?

Andrea Brady

Export Zone

Showing the slit across the thigh, she anchors
the erotic by which burundi girls buy un
hcr relief. Is that enough milk
foaming venus blood shot through narrow arteries
sewn up with grass and thorn. Exotic
            imports unsold sweating
bushmeat, a race for extinction won at the starting
gun. Every tactic is neurotic, down to the wire

down to the long nail. Before the noon bulletin
I've sucked off two enemies and crossed
my arms over my mouth demand for
beauty on the bell curve, ringing
            the change is slight on a five pound note.

And the sign for *abcde* is camp
catastrophics, the cash transfer from london
lite to salt lick has some chick as its
sole beneficiary. Would I like her
whipped or salted
the critical assessments are in
the latest colour, mocha grande.

I sat in front of the terminal bowed by
happy news. He's coming, down the basra
            highway the eastern mainline toppling regime
intimacy fabricated across brand loyalty makes
the sky whipped to spreadable cloud, how long

to the end of sacrifice, how to hold breaths and forbear
relief until just then. The privilege of
purchase on one life, no matching gifts programme
can convince the easter season opens
            laying out purple and pink under bowed branches.

Doctors refuse to look at a local sample, even these
lines sucked tight as zippers betray
their sex with pink flapping. How to feel
pleasure when writing is a work of repressive
sympathy, how do you celebrate time?

Ian Burnette

Dutch Baby

In the bakery, my girl
grips a pregnancy test

like a pistol in her pocket.
The baker hands her

the key to the restroom
and leaves. In the back

there's a small window
where he watches

men and women and
children – I don't mind,

I've learned I can't
protect anyone by now.

The raspberry danish
in the pastry cabinet

is the baker's daughter,
I've decided – bruised

purple and swaddled
in puff rope. I imagine

the baker coming back
from his window, filling

my empty hands.
Here's yeast, here's flour,

fruit and sugar and water –
make more of her.

Brendan Cleary

It's Our Dance

for Lorna

Every Sunday
I play Nina Simone's
'My baby just cares for me'
& with a different flower
in your hair every week
you spring out from the bar
& I leave the mixing desk
& we dance with our hangovers,
yes we dance around the bar
& last week we ended up
outside briefly on Lewes Road
in the petrol hazes
& we even waltzed
out to the beer garden
& everybody smiles
when we dance together
to 'My baby just cares for me'
& for a few precious minutes
it's as if we have all swallowed the moon
& everyone is lighter
& the world might not ever end.

Graham Clifford

The Best Poem Ever Written

I write a poem that is the best. Massive.
Not just long, but huge intellectually
and although it is book length
reading is like freefalling,
each line greased with two genius thoughts.

The poem makes me famous.
I wander oxygen-depleted nights
down city streets and hear
lines of my poem bartered
between sticky lovers.

On the train, I peek over the top
of a hardback book about me
at a man in a suit nodding off
and recognise the words he's mouthing in his swoon.

All front pages, every day,
showcase stanzas of my poem –
bombings and murders get tucked inside.
The new novelist pays well
to get my poem printed as an introduction:
she knows her work makes no sense without it.

Everyone I have ever known
rings me to ask how I did it.
I say I don't know, and that's the truth.
After a year the fuss hasn't died away.

I sit at my computer
and hear next door turn the TV on.
I put my ear to the wall.
It's an actor and he's reading my poem.
It's a good version: I've heard it before.

He has a Shakespearean voice
doing justice to what the introducer called
The Best Poem Ever Written.
I listen to it all, I travel where the poem takes me
then get back in my chair
and write a better one.

David Constantine

The Rec

Back home and finding the rec gone
Flogged off, become a gated community
CCTV in every hanging basket
And identical shaven-headed fat men
Aiming remotes each at his own portcullis

How can I make of it a 'luminous emptiness'
As Heaney did of his axed chestnut tree?
It's a space stuffed full with hardware
Loungers and meat. At thirty paces
It lights up sodium white. Pitbulls prowl the wire.

Oh that man who stands at the bus-stop all day long
And whatever number bus comes he never gets on
But tells everybody waiting, It was all fields round here
When I was a boy – day by day, more and more
He's me. I tell them Miss Eliza Smythe left the rec

In trust to the Town in perpetuity
For the health of children, her line dying out.
It was an old enclosure quick-set with hawthorn
And we lay there watching and waiting for our turn
In a team-game on the free ground under the open sky.

Only the moon and stars lit up the rec.
Few still believe there was such a playing-place
But, yes, another elegy would be very nice
So remember all you like. Can we live on lack?
Should have stopped them grabbing it. Should take it back.

Robert Crawford

Herakleitos

eftir Kallimachos

Herakleitos,
Whan they telt me
Ye'd deed
Wey bak,
I grat,
Mindin
Yon nicht
We sat oot gabbing
Till the cauld
Peep o day.
An sae, ma auld
Halikarnassian pal,
Ye got seik
And noo ye're someplace
Deid in the grun –
But thae sangs, aa
Yon nichtingales o yourn,
Still soun
Lik they sounded
Then
When we set oot
An sat oot,
Twa young men.
Daith taks the lot,
They sey,
But, ach,
Thae sangs
He's nivver
Gonnae get.

in memory of Mick Imlah

telt told; *deed* died; *grat* wept; *gabbing* talking; *peep o day* dawn; *seik* ill; *grun* ground; *yourn* yours; *soun* sound

Theodore Deppe

Shouting at the Windows of the Night
2 November 1965

My *birthday of the electric guitar*. It might for me
have been nothing more than the four of us
practising in the basement, *Louie Louie*

because our governor tried to ban the song statewide,
thereby proclaiming it *the* anthem any Indiana band
must learn first. Johnny claimed

he knew the real version, lyrics so lewd
the Kingsmen had to slur them, so we mastered the art
of mumbling the words meaningfully.

Then someone said we'd never beat the government
in making the obscene unclear,
so in that not-quite soundproof cellar –

until Father came down to say, *Boys,*
it's a school night – we shouted the wrong words
to *Louie Louie* as clearly as we could.

I didn't hear the news until later, but the same day
I turned fifteen a Quaker from Baltimore
drove through rush-hour red to the Pentagon.

Witnesses disagreed whether Norman Morrison
doused himself in kerosene before or after
he let his infant daughter go, but she was there

as her father became a twelve-foot pillar of fire
roaring at the window of the Defense Secretary.
And no one – not the bystanders, not the police

who rushed to his side,
not Secretary McNamara himself –
no one could make out his last words.

Forty-four birthdays ago, but sometimes
Norman Morrison still draws near
as I celebrate. He who had done

everything he knew how to do – protested, prayed,
refused war taxes – now shares with me
the second of November, the Day of the Dead.

Something in me thinks I understand
giving one's life for others, but what if he meant
to take his daughter with him, what if he thought

an American child must burn
so we would see what napalm does?
The flames rose and at some point this father

let his daughter go. Perhaps he held her
until his arm muscles contracted in a jolt of flame,
or maybe an angel commanded, *Release her*,

though I hope he'd already put her down,
before lighting the match, knowing
this death was his alone.

Witnesses could tell us nothing. They only agreed
they couldn't understand a single word
he shouted at the windows of the night.

Imtiaz Dharker

Talker

When there is no-one else close by
to talk to, you have this habit
of speaking to yourself.
I can hear you out in the workshop,
talking to a motorbike or to its wheels,
scolding a stubborn saw or drill.

When you sit up in the study
poring over papers in the night
I sometimes hear you discussing
(I think with your first, dead wife)
the question of insurance and electric bills.

Once or twice I have caught sight of you
walking down the street alone,
your mouth moving and your hand replying,
because the conversation once begun
must take its course till it is done,

and every night before the clock strikes one,
over the radio's monotone, you tell me
our whole day from start to end, how we woke
and where we walked, how the time unfolded
like an origami bird

till we came home to bed, hand in hand,
past the shivering queue of Saturday girls
with pale legs and brave faces, their teeth
chattering, their words hung in front of their mouths
as if they were only talking to themselves.

Douglas Dunn

Guyane

An Indian archer poses in nine colours
On a ridge, he draws his bow, his body arched
As a visible echo of bowstring and curve.
This valley can be blue-green, lilac-rose,
Red-orange or sepia. Colour-changes on
Little pictures accord with value, oxidization,
And with imagined places. Rapids shot
By three men in a canoe mean green water,
Rose-carmine, brown, or blue. Earlier issues
Depict anteaters, gold washers, and coconut palms –
Beautiful snapshots of remote, hot peace,
For some, and how colonial business earns its whack.
Prisoners on Devil's Island, licking the gum –
Assuming they were allowed to write home,
Assuming they could write – might have found it
Too close for comfort to the taste of freedom
And a normal life. Ditto the garrison,
Their sweltering wives. The 1947
And final issues show a hammocked woman –
Repos guyanais, meaning 'the natives are lazy' –
A pirogue on the Maroni approaching a village,
A similar design, but by the banks of the Oyapok
Up-country in Inini, then a Guyanaise
In fetching straw millinery, followed by
Toucans, macaws, a pair of big eagles,
An aeroplane over palms and a peccary,
Cuvier's toucan and a black-necked aracan.
My father pushed philately as 'educational'.
Only if discontent can teach anything.
Only if possession soothes discontent.
Only if discontent becomes passion.
Only if passion doesn't overstep
Rules of behaviour and become obsession.
Now, permutate the infinities of 'only if'.

Josh Ekroy

Guided Tour

Come with me my friend, come English,
mind your step in this street, he is Shia,
no-one can move him. The Mujahideen want
him to rot in front of his family
in his dirty track suit and broken sandals.
Look how those women turn from the dried blood.

The Shia are cunning and have thicker blood,
Sunnis have hooded eyes and move, English,
with their feet flapping their sandals.
Look at that man, he is certainly a Shia,
you can tell from his shouting family.
Now we leave Mu'alemeen Street. If you want

to visit this morgue, you will also want
a nose tissue because there is stink of blood.
Forty bodies come in – three families.
They have been tortured and dumped, English,
sometimes in the sewage plant, the Shias
float in that black canal with rotting sandals.

The mourners also are attacked, their sandals
stolen too, so their restless fingers want
the cool steel of triggers when they leave Shia
area because they have bad blood
towards Sunni. Behind these blast blocks, English,
they see who is friend, who is family.

Here at this barred window, whole families
lean over shoulders, count sandals.
Look, come here. You can see the clerk, English,
with computer, he does not really want
to show on his screen the pools of blood
for these people at the bars, the Shia.

Come, you can see the dead faces of the Shia
if you stand on your toes – that family
is all wiped out – you can observe black blood
and purple bruises and the tattered sandal.
Come, there is a beggar who is never free from want,
and here are the kids with pistols, English!

The English – do they like to take care of family?
Shia is shamed, if they do not. Remove sandals,
this Mosque requires it. Now we are one blood.

Carrie Etter

Imagined Sons 9: Greek Salad

For a week I travel on business, and on the fourth afternoon, I go to a restaurant to have yet another meal alone. I order a Greek salad and read a Dickens novel to escape my loneliness.

When the salad arrives, I barely look. How will Jenny Wren respond to news of her drunken father's death? I push the fork into the lettuce, and it yields slowly to the tines. The balance of balsamic vinegar and olive oil, with the sweetness of the red lettuce, is perfect, and I pause, relishing the flavour.

I hear the smallest of shrieks. I think I must have anticipated Jenny, that I must have been that engrossed, when I hear it again. I put my book down so its open pages press the plastic tablecloth and keep my place, and my fork dives again, spearing a cube of feta.

'Stop! Stop!' The sound rises from the salad.

'Who – what are you?' I whisper. '*Where* are you?'

A black olive wiggles atop a romaine leaf, as though to wave. 'I am your son, brutally transformed!'

I glance around the restaurant and see the other diners, all in groups, engaged in conversation. 'When I last saw you, you were an infant. How did you get into this state?' I say with some sharpness.

I think I see him cringe. Meekly, he says, 'I fell in love with the virgin mistress of the god's own olive grove. When I made love to her, I was turned into an olive tree!'

'When you made love to her?'

The softest of whispers: '*They* say, when I raped her.'

'So you are a tree as well as this olive?' I ask, trying to move my mouth as little as possible as I see the waiter coming from the kitchen. 'So she tends to you, there in the grove?'

'She only knows I disappeared,' the olive whines. 'She tends to me, yes, but without thought, without love. It is a fate worse than –'

'Delicious,' I say to the waiter, swallowing the small olive whole. 'Just delicious.'

John Foggin

Camera Obscura

(Emily Wilding Davison. June 1913)

The reason for your being here
is out of sight. They can't be seen –
your Cause's colours sewn inside
your decent coat: white, violet, green.

The camera sees the moment
you began to die:
the jockey, trim in silks, is doll-like
on the grass and seems asleep;
his mount is spraddled on its back;
its useless hooves flail at the sky.

Your spinning, flower-trimmed hat
is stopped, distinct, mid-flight;
your hair's still not come down;
you're frozen, inches from the ground;
your boots are neatly buttoned,
take small steps on the arrested air.

You're stopped in time. No sound,
no texture, no sour odour
of bruised grass and earth. Just
silence and the alchemy of light.

How did you comprehend
the shock of heat, huge muscle, hair,
in that white moment
when the dark came down?

The camera cannot tell;
its business neither truth nor lies.
It shows a fallen horse. A woman falling. A crowd

in hats and blazers staring down a long perspective;
the field intent upon the distant fairy icing
grandstand. The waving flags. The finish line.

Until the image blurs, dissolves in silver flowers,
it's there on celluloid in shades of grey;
the camera only says that in that instant
you are dying, and everyone has looked away.

SJ Fowler

Trepidation

don't change the plans at the last minute so that each person who
makes up the room
that is this room who was come to be defined by that which they
came here to watch
may quickly find that I don't think as much as I should about their
being in love
with their work colleague or neighbour for I am not so timid as
not to say
anything about that and change that which particularly concerns
me within
the compass of this lesson that is here to be allowed in Berlin
where I am to speak from the centre of a language while my dance
partner will
offer me a mattress of paper which floats about our nervous chats
so that I may speak clearly in an Nglish that you all understand
& of course you have come to know a journey to be here through
the snow
and didn't imagine you would face a motion that might be dance
and is not the practise
of tactile familiarity to throw or trip another human body to the
floor
to end up beneath or to deflect the swing of a knife which you
have no chance of deflecting
and then an address of that journey you undertook in gratitude
pleased to be indifferent to how we have been sought out
when of course but not considered there are things at play which
you cannot know
in my experience over the last five days since I have been here in
Berlin
knowing this performance would come & no doubt you have read
your textbooks
from the guild of a dance company that lives in a prison is just a
moments' walk away

and we have all here visited that website which offers opinions
on whether I personally should invest in property in Neukolln or
Wedding
yeayou laugh   as if it were possible in this city   that someone who
is addressing
your journey as though it were the subject for poetry could have
enough money
to also own property even in a place as cheap as one that has no
readily available work
for the iron women on rudy dutschke that are pretending to wear
the full hijab
and walk five steps behind me but listen carefully and you can
hear their tools
being readied by the striking of a clock in the night's deserted
hours around here
where there are no nightclubs no bars no ready alcohol and from
my high window
as if in a poor painting of a singing voice being strangled in the
past I have the cold
blown upon my fingers and realise in these words like a child
that it's a shame for my first lesson to point out that good things
happen for bad reasons

Tom French

The Delivery Room

James Henry French, b. 20.11.2003

They had wheeled your mother to theatre
in a plunge-back gown for the performance
of a lifetime, and left us to keep company
at her bedside after the bed was gone –

you on the flat of your back in an incubator,
a spaceman, minutes old, taking it all in
and taking your time about sampling the air.
Someone is going to tell you, so let it be me –

because the blood and the heat were too much
I lifted the sash window and, slipping my head out
for a breath of air, took in the cemetery – the skip
parked inside the gate for withered wreaths,

the far corner, filled with innocents, still green,
row upon row of neat marble and granite,
the only sound a car on the Bridge of Peace
and an ambulance idling at A&E.

We will never be in a room as full or as empty.
The first voices we heard were voices off –
night sisters whispering, nearing their shift's end,
that the night just gone had felt like an eternity.

Jen Hadfield

Definitions

after Jerome Rothenberg

The Brisket
This cinched consonant, hunched muscle in a yellow
simmet, could also signify a journey. It could feed a family,
or stop the third gob of the three-headed dog. You bind it
to your stick as you set off for the Underworld. Browned, it
melts into punctuated mud, is thick fuel for migrations,
night flights you can't remember. It's a passing madness in
the cat; it makes him a round-eyed bawling bob-cat. It
squirms under the distal phalanges of a splayed hand. It
bucks the bite of the knife. It foams fat.

The Cat
is sleeping very deeply now it's spring been off his head
hunting rabbits all night, in the far-out stones and discoball
eyes of the clifftop crö. His days a kind of stoned remission:
heart-beat irregular, muscles leaping violently in sleep. The
wet bracelet of his mouth unlatched; chattering a little; his
eyelids half-open. His furry buffers nicely spread all about
him; nicely buffered by fat and fur all round.

Equus Primus
as if some god having turned out another batch of
underdone horses (thin as leaves, dappled like leaves) freed
them on the hill to flicker like a thicket of hornbeam and
willow; set down his cutter and balled the waste dough.
Thence this tribe of blackened emoticons, tough as plugs.

The Word 'Died'
It's a cliff-sided stack: sheer, almost an island. A human
can't stand upon that high, tilted pasture but life crowds its
cliffs: sheep and nesting maas, the waste-not plants of
heath and moor. You hear the waves breaking but can't see
them. You shrink down into yourself as you reach the edge:
getting your head around where you are. It's marvellous.
It's aweful. It is always on. Like a massive *and* unfolding its
wings, and mantling. It was here all along, reached by
Shirva and the derelict mills; turf sweating in the hot,
midgy smirr.

The Mackerel
At once, the three hooks chime. The skin is as supple as the
skin on boiled milk and the eye a hard, roundel pane. It is
or it isn't wormy, it tastes of hot blood and earth, tastes of
long-awaited rain, winter lightning and summer thunder.
Heart-throb; mud-coloured; the cooked flesh is tarnish. The
oatmeal crisp. It tastes of steak, it tastes of cream.

The Northern Lights
– but yes, now you pull over – after the headlights, a raw
shifting glare. I've taken them often for a moon behind
cloud. An ambiguous rustling, yes, maybe listening in, when
being overheard is your greatest fear. Like an infection of the
lymph, a shooting-up – that single, white flare.

The Orange
Bloated, swollen with sea-water, it's a boast, fraught with
salt syrup. It forces your fingers apart and makes much of
itself. It is über, *aaber.* A very straining round real orange,
stinking of orange and the sea; stinking of stale cologne.
The sea returns whatever you give it, more so, realler.
Headachy wax! It rolls down the sand into the foam. It
spins at the crest of the breaker!

The Parents
are on the pale brisk longbusy birdbrushed billows of the equinoctial sea. Without them is a long, unhappy holiday. Who else gives a shit about your shitty knee? You're breathless at the thought of them all-night on the sea. Blithely they step into its bright pale machinery. They make mandalas of quartz and limpet-shells, hide cash under a hairbrush, vanish with their luggage as pixies might. The pillows squared to each other. The sheets pulled tight.

The Pig
is as they say, very human, though our bellies do not resemble her belly, which is like one of the papyriform columns at Luxor. Nor can we liken our nipples to her torment of buttons, our ears to her arums. Our lugs are unfringed with soft, blonde baleen. But her fetishes: her forked stick; her devilish loop of rotted rope. Her precious rasher of chicken wire. Her tired, human eye. Her constancy as a conspirator.

The Puffballs
Somebody's watching. Two toughened eyeballs propped behind you on the turf.

The Puffin
A tangled marionette, strings of jerked sinew. Summer's end, the derelict burrow, a ring of dirty down. An arabesque of smelly bone, meat for flies and the darling turf. The head may be full of meat; the large beak, faded: a Fabergé egg.

The Road to the North Light
It weeps tar from tender parts like frogskin. Thin, mobile
muscles squirm under your soles as it bears you across the
Hill Dyke on a current of cool air, the bed of an invisible
river. It has heather and tormentil, not dandelion but catsear.
It has a creep over a precipice; it has sorrel, parched and tiny.
It carries you above the white and lilac sea; it switchbacks,
and turns you before the sun like a sacrifice.

The Slater
We alone among the creatures are known to imagine our
own minds. Like this woodlouse on the kitchen floor. It
perceives you, rears and comes about. Stroking with its
spurred feet a precipitate of dried soup, a peel hovering
above its own shadow.

The Waxcaps
Someone was carried across this field, bleeding steadily.

David Harsent

Fire: a Song for Mistress Askew

fythynesse, rust, menstrue, swylle, mannys durt, adders egges, the brede of lyes…

Johan Bayle

The firebug rises whistling from the fire. Slats laid
on the overlap, branches at a pitch, as for Anne Askew
wordless under torture, so broken the hangman's crew
carried her to the stake, a seat where she sat astride.

It has come to this. Bramble and thorn,
lumber and junk. Dead stuff. Whatever would burn.

*

Charge and denial; the bald accounts of martyrdom;
the mechanics at work, their gift of transformation.
Torchlight and stone. She stripped to her shift
unbidden and climbed up to the machine; when it took hold
she was lifted clear of the bed, her body hard strung,
the wrench and crack of greenstick.

Notebook: *She bell'd*
but speke no worde and sylence alwayes her gift.

*

The frame of her in the fire, black to the bone. Her head
a smoking cinder, smiling, smiling, smiling.
Some stood close enough to catch the haul
and roar of flame in the summer wind as it fed,
close enough to hear the shrivel-hiss
of burning hair, to see her sag and slump, to witness
the pucker and slide of her skin, the blister-rash on her eyeballs.

In the fire lies your salvation, Anne, they said. What greater thing
than the brush of His hand as He stoops to take up your soul?

*

Notebook: (*Her Newgate poem*) –
A woman poore and blinde:
more enmyes now I have than hairs upon my hedd.
(She stood her ground.)
Then the byshopp sayd, I shuld be brente.

*

Anne, you are nothing to me. Only that you knew best
how to unfasten your gown while they waited at the rack.
Only that *she was hard prest*
which I can't now shake from my mind. Only that black
flux flowed from you, that they let you void and bleed.

*

I set this fire in a hard frost: early evening, the garden's
winter leavings, the unretrievable, the piecemeal burdens.
Paraffin to start it – that dry *whoomph!* – and I saw her ghost
chained there: the woodcut from Foxe's 'Acts
and Monuments' that hung on the chapel wall
beside 'The Light of the World', a mild-mannered Christ,
his jaunty crown of thorns... The minister's stage-effects
were rage and unforgiveness, his colours red and red again
which were heart's blood and hell-fire, the least of us already lost.

*

Notebook: *(Johan Bayle, her apologist)* –
By the fore heades understande she the hartes
or myndes of men. (And then): Christ wuld speake

in darke symylytudes. (And of her judges): They brede
cockatrice egges and weve the spyders webbe.

*

That they gave her cripple-water; that she ate
spoiled meat; that this was her penance; that she saw
those long nights through bedded on stone and straw;
that women in the garden by the White Tower,
turned to one another, amazed: '*What is that animal?*'
The river beat,
hour after hour as they racked her, back from the water gate.

*

That job taken in hand by Wriothesley and Richard Rich.
Then the pyre at Smithfield; those there to watch:
Norfolk, Bonner, Bowes, priests, judges, one and all
the Devil's dishwashers. Before they lit the stack,
Shaxton preached repentance. Broken, she listened.
The crowd stood round in a ring, ten deep, and felt the scorch.

*

Notebook: *(Johan Bayle, in sorrow)* –
So had Anne Askewe the flamynge brandes of fyre,
nor scremed until the first flaym reched her brest.

*

My dream of her puts me in close-by: her poor bare
feet, her shift just catching a flame that chases the line of the hem …
And when I wake in sunlight, that flare is the flare
in her eye, that rising note in my ear the singing deep in green
branches, that low rumble her blood at a rolling boil;
and what she screams from the centre, now, as her hair
goes up in a rush, as her fingers char,

as the spit on her tongue bubbles and froths, as she browns from heel
to head, as she cracks and splits, as she renders to spoil:
the only thing she can get to me through the furnace, as I lean
in to her, is *yes it will be fire it will be fire it will be fire…*

Lee Harwood

Naming the Names

Sailing across the bay to the outer islands,
a bright blustery day (I imagine this), and
all the pain of history just blows away.

Shall we have white sails? or blue? or Brixham red?
And back in the harbour the masts crowd together.
'Blue Shadow', 'Red Duster', 'Imfrey', 'Lumpy Custard'.

At night a drift of clouds, but the stars so bright –
Orion's Belt, The Plough, maybe The Little Dipper.
The flash of a distant lighthouse. Beyond this… it wavers.
And in the city?

Back and forth across the oceans to those continents
cluttered with so much stuff, whether it be simply
shoes and plates, books and pictures, or not so simply.

As the years pass so lost at times in those familiar streets.
A weight of memories, or just another
casual bombing and strafing raid across the Channel.

Did you know what was happening then? A child
who's taken to see where the V1 rocket landed,
where a row of six houses had disappeared.

At such a distance there's no knowing except
the sound of crunching glass as you're carried
across the bedroom, window blown in across the bed,

that's always remembered. In a quiet room somewhere,
sunlight and...   On the spread-out map
all the gradations of blue.

Amazed at the colours

for Robert Vas Dias on his 80th birthday

Colin Herd

Rug Design

it's going to be
elliptical, the
background in
porcelain white.
around the edges
there'll be grey
patches and
splodges like
residual debris.
the odd faintly
outlined schools
or families of
bubbles in a
lighter grey a
little further in,
some hugging
each other, conjoined
together, others
fending for themselves,
out on their own.
about 35cms from
the right hand
point and 20
in from the edge,
there'll be a silvery
rectangle with
one of its edges folded
in on itself, the folded
edge will be red.
within the silver bit,
there are hints
of apricot, just
traces. then, about

a further 20 cm over
there will be three
largish irregular
clouds of the same
apricot, maybe a little
less pastel, a little
more sherbert. the
shape doesn't
matter too much
as long as they are
irregular, maybe
base one on a wall-
mounted vincent
fecteau sculpture,
another on one of
those foam pointing
hands you get at
sports grounds and
the final one should
be like a flat pool,
shoe-insole-shape.
that's about it. the
concept of the design
is based on my sink-
soap dish, which
spoke to me this
morning while i
was brushing my
teeth.

Caoilinn Hughes

Gathering Evidence

He would have been a fan of Newton, the householder
who guzzled his millet gruel and malt beer one bitter
morning in Wales and ran outside to capture hailstones.

'An extraordinary Shower of Hail,' he recorded, 'broke down
the stalks of all the beans and wheat… and ruined as much glass
at Major Hansbury's House as cost 4 pounds the repairing.'

'Some of the Hail were 8 inches about; as to their Figure,
very irregular and unconstant, several of the Hail-stones being
compounded, as the Major judged, who saw them.'

He wore nothing more than rhinegrave breeches
gathered at the knee, garterless stockings, vestless
but for a ruffled shirt – slashed sleeves furled, meaning business.

Gravity had been newly named, so he willed himself to see
the hail as being drawn, not thrown forcefully from the Heavens.
The orbs burst on the ground like meteors or fleshy white melons.

To measure their diameter before they dissolve is to grasp
the hard idea before the thawing thought, he held. If he could secure
a hailstone in a wheelbarrow, with solid algebra, he could square a
circle.

To square a circle! He might as well have measured the Garden
of Eden if he could master this binomial expansion. He handled
the pellets like enormous diamonds: what could they reveal? The
world

was so full of revelation in those days. One could drop a needle
in a haystack and pinpoint the magnetic field. One could begin a
conversation.
He looked at the frozen rain and saw concentric rings as in an
axed tree;

he swallowed one like a lozenge, half-hoping a golden band would
be left
on his tongue, half-not. His wife pleaded him in to safety. He was
ecstatic.
He bellowed how the stones had wed through their seven-mile drop.

What did that mean? His evidence was dissolving; the ghoulish
green sky,
lightening. He had not been stunned. He had felt the world upon
him,
but the welts it left would not be proof enough. As the Major judged,

if the fellow could only have captured a skyful, he could have
squared it.
The esteemed witness was vital. Else, all he would have been
left with was a wife who would not nurse his fever, and indefinite
vital signs.

Alexander Hutchison

Adrift is Maybe Not the Word

We were all attempting to avoid
damp patches, spent matches, old
snatches that couldn't raise a smile.
We were all vainly scraping around
for scant reward. No sap, no savour.
Song and 'puff' was all we had to
go on now. Plum duff or porridge
in a drawer would not sustain us.

We were all hoping for something
better, to put it frankly; something
we could all get stuck properly into:
mulch and compost, deep-cut ditches.
Fibrillators, respirators maybe not.
Flint-glance or twirling to conjure a
spark. Zygotes and teeny brain cells
brought extravagantly into play.

We were all maybe looking for
something that wasn't there, or
couldn't be touched, didn't exist.
Brisk, complex – or *un*complicated,
who's to say? Who's to hear?
Rope on, lighten up. Feel that? It's
whoa on the one hand, *whoa*, *whoa*;
on the other restive, omnivorous.

Gavia Stellata

Who calls to the dark?
Who, when the shadows
are converted to morning,
when light pours out, when
day is turned to darkness
once more, when dark
is on the face of the sea,
who dives down, who
brings back a speck
to build on? I do. I did.

Who is the smallest
and brightest
and speckled
with stars? I am.

All things that gather
to shine I bear on my back
I raise on my wings
in the black of the waters,
in the deep vault of space.

Who dips and dives?
Dense bones take me down.

Who rose with a twin,
with another, who breasted
the face of the night, who
stitched the belt of stars
in Orion? Who speeds
without drag: bill like an awl
and flattened tarsus, neatest
and fleetest in streamlined

propulsion? Who took
Arcturus like a morsel of light,
a pinch of snuff, returned
to the surface?

Who calls to the dark,
who calls to the wind on
the surface of the water?
Who prompts the others
to dip and rise? Eyes like
seeds of garnet. Lightest
and brightest: *gavia stellata*
the red-throated diver.

August Kleinzahler

Epistle xxxix

Aggrievius, how is it that I'm certain that you, no other,
will be the one to speak most eloquently at my memorial?
Because it is you, dear friend, who best husbanded
kind remarks of any sort, and, likewise, praise, in life,
the better that it might gush forth now in a single, extravagant go.
There you are, struggling, fighting back your grief. It's evident
to everyone on hand: the strangled, staccato bursts,
the troubled breathing. Hang in there, old son, you've rehearsed
too long and hard to get tangled up in sentiment now.
There, there, you're beginning to calm down. We're all relieved,
even me, and I'm dead. Behold, Aggrievius, in full sail,
canvas snapping in the wind as we approach his peroration.
It's true, you know, I really was a decent chap, underneath:
kind to dogs, shop clerks – and something of a wit, to boot.
You trot out a few of my *bons mots* to make that very point, suggesting
that my more fierce or pungent asides are better left shelved
for now. – *Ho, ho, ho*, the assembled murmur, demurely.
A few of the best were at your expense, but we'll let that go.
You would have filed in, the lot of you, to Biber's *Rosary Sonatas*,
the Crucifixion part, 'Agony in the Garden,' all that.
Hardly the soundtrack, one would have guessed, for an old, dead Jew.
Quite a few of these chicks on hand have it going on still, eh?
You'd really have to blow it big time not to get laid,
what with all the tears, perfume, black lace... Am I being awful?
Forgive me. But it is my party, after all. *After all*, after all.
I'd say, on balance, it was a very nice show. In fact,
I might as well have scripted it myself, perhaps with better pacing.
But I could not have improved upon your speech, Aggrievius, no.
It really is you, finally, who knew me best and loathed me most.

Martin Kratz

The Man Who Walked Through Walls

To walk through walls
into a vault or out of a cell
the criminal, John Dillinger,
simply placed his palms
against the cool-skinned plaster

and pushed with enough force
for his body to sieve through
the concrete in a single
steady motion and pool
together on the other side.

He couldn't put his finger
on exactly what happened
inside the stone, anymore
than he could put his finger
on exactly the point at which

he fell from being awake to asleep:
all the spaces in the wall filled
with John Dillinger, all the spaces
in Dillinger filled with wall,
and there was no John Dillinger.

There was no
Man Who Walked Through Walls.
No man who learned too well
what it meant to be Inside,
what it really meant to be Out,

and that Inside was filled
with Out and Outside
filled with In, like a wall
filled with John Dillinger,
a Dillinger filled with wall.

When they shot the criminal,
John Dillinger, he looked
like a human colander.
But they couldn't shoot the
Man Who Walked Through Walls,

the man who came at the stone
one last time, with enough
momentum to see himself
begin but not complete
what he started –

into the wall but not out.
Or neither In nor Out.
Or maybe to say, he finally
put his finger on the point
at which he fell asleep.

Hannah Lowe

The Other Family

The boy blows bubbles
at the camera in a garden
of yellow roses,
then the woman blows them,
then the boy.
You tumble up
from a fake fall, your jaw
meeting the boy's fist,
his arms flailing wildly,
you unfurling punches
that don't connect,
don't come close to that,
dancing backwards on your toes
to the kitchen door.
This is years ago,
the woman at the sink
in an orange dress,
her hands lost in the suds,
watching the man and boy spar,
the man teaching the boy
how to be a man, the boy
recalling a bubble's
holographic light, or upstairs,
the box room with its
wallpaper of blue trains
where he woke early to a spot
of sunlight on the skirting board
which made him think
of birds or god

until he heard your key
click in the door.
And the woman downstairs
stacking dishes, thinking
of the night she woke in,
moonlight sliced across
the rug, the empty space
beside her, not knowing
where you were.
This is years ago.
The camera has stopped rolling
but we are spinning back,
frame by frame,
the boy, the woman,
you – driving in your car,
driving miles, all night,
with money in your pocket,
coming home
with what you know.

Seán Lysaght

Storm Diary

Wind from the east is a banshee wailing
at the door, from the west a howling chimney.
The worst nights, the car is tense as a cat.
The two of us are there at the centre
of force nines shaking the gate and rattling
the loose slates of our insistence:
we have made the right choice. Hours of telly,
journal entries, phone calls from outside
pass our time in the lighthouse with a query
(even as the whitethorns I planted knuckle
down and shy away from standing straight).
How many winters before our hearts are
twisted? And the wind answers: by the time
you know that, it will already be too late.

Lydia Macpherson

Lithium Lovesong

My element, seamed in stone
and tethered now between helium
and beryllium, a foil balloon pulling
at your moorings, your supple almostness
fingers gravity, kissing air and blackening
with it. As hard to cut as moonlight,
you're pulling me like a tide away
from knife drawers and cliff edges,
safety-netting my amygdala.

Unmaddened and inhibited,
I pop your blisterpacks like bladderwrack,
put on your drugged armour like some new crustacean.
You are the lulling surf in my heartbeat,
the ozone in my metalled mouth,
the wavering in my fingertip: take me
to the smooth sea's bed and tie me down,
wrap me up tight and level me,
let me learn to live a flattened life.

Lorraine Mariner

Strangers

Those people who talk
to strangers
who make eye contact
with absolutely anyone –

their souls have a lid
perhaps or lashes
some form of protection
because most people

are not to be trusted
and how do they cope
with the brightness
when they are?

Ian McEwen

Father Lost Lost

1

and here bent forward at the Wind insensible in this world as through Glass he Hauls, become mere hauling

and it's another Poem of Dead Dads or dads not dead but blown against their Absence like stock metaphor that drip Drip drips – the family Photo and how the Mower rusted stiff over its Butterfly of oil distils a sepia tincture in the garage – a concrete Stain and the paint does never cover

and the Volume on the Telly stuck at full on Daytime jokes/ disasters all as squashy as the Sofas like that Cowboy torture where they cut the Lids away and soon enough he cannot see – now must this Wind still wear upon the Ears

and *Macula*, that Spot original and growing as the Bubble break and tear and blow the surfaces away to What was never always there Degenerate in this world every loss leads into never finished Constant Present, new tense he taps into forward: always ahead

his small Tent far out upon the Ice – and this Wind

2

which is the stick you Stuck with stuck the wrong stick in the Stick-stand or standing at a standstill, Too Short she says, the stick girl and it's underStandable but here you stick and Make a stand

which is the penitent, the Christmas film, Bent as that man slipped Under blades and Bend you to remain, tapping Forward ticking forward, tipping forward One stick at a time against This breath this gale insensible, reflected on the glass as all the lost ark of your head Bent and the ground

which is become a Punctuation, pause, the tap of Stick the stuck of breath the stiffened arc of Back turned like a mark invented to pretend pretend that each Half finished thing is

which is the bow the bowe the Bark of bowow time is pulling taut the tendon shortens Ticking as the span pulls In a sinking or a tension fit to launch

sticks Lately after us Which is more Useable than bones

3

where is each second Kicking him with Offbeats vicious in The heart insists Insists it Can in peevish opposition tense against the Dark the Bed the push placed wrong

where there's No righting the lopsiding Mop of pillows Dad cranes forward from His His Bed the frame the life he won't lie back on Forward the wrong accent in this clinic clinical clinic, the cardiac that Kicks him and the can All down

where there is a Mop to push, a mop that clangs against the Can, a day job and a night job but no second Dark not really and the shock is Bars across a window in the pastel care and there is no is Not escape where the Mop Mop moping of the heart goes Forward

where our lopsided Clocks are strewn and Tock Tock Tock not ticking proper but it's the beat you stick with and where God is but a better Ear than us had better be a better Ear

and blowing comes Stravinsky where his Stethoscope

4

as the survivor Bound to paths to lists the ark of Clocks that wind and Wind that ticks the clicking in the paper house Insists the ear insists the post and Taps that drip and paint and stain insists on still these Hills

as the Survivor bound to concrete As in forms to fill And files to find to fix in mind the game the objects, sticks and Paints, Insists on pillows mowers, spots stuck on Petals, hills, to correspondence by the Clocks and ticks to bills and with the hills inside the Glass

as the Survivor bound to logic, stuck held or pretended that A scope A variable hope A bound A limp A lope blown Lopsided forward into logic Bent and tapping towards trope

as the survivor Bound to find The form to haul the line to Form the plot To fix the Drip to Stick The Paper butterflies all in

and only to survive

5

and Who behind the glass all dripping Supercooled, bent and hauled, that bows and bowes the present Past the penitence of hills and who

and who Takes it to tick and tock and Drip and drop that cardiac Caress, the flapping tent of chest, that heart unfortified and Butterflied from routine beauty morning Duty in your nature in the Dark and who

and who for What we know Why should We retrograde in going Back to school among the beds and sofas you Must Know your father any the most vulgar thing to sense whose Common theme is: flourish, exeunt all but, who and who upon this Spot lopsided broken Butterfly along the row, the Daddy cabbages of hope, it shows a will the Stick and net contraption the Wind tears and wears and where we stop and Mop and Hoe and Hoo

who Still hath cried a Fault against the Dead and who

6

one is the Echo of the street at four, the Bell and after as kids drift, small growlers into Evening polyester blue, and finished, stopped, the wind is like the Bell at four o'clock you find it when it is never finished in the Ear

one is the Petal turned lopsided, bent on the carpet, geranium, the fade making the picture just as any three points plot a curve and where His hills line up all afternoon or we pretend the hills

one is or two just One or Two the breaking little flakes their metal Butterflies and each one different the same, pepper the green, Mop into stone, come, become and unbecome in Dark

one is the bird that starts it now, no sleep for That one optimist deluded in the Dark that just One day from solstice must be and is at least one thing to Sing for, optimist

and Early better than One second Late

Hubert Moore

Hosing Down

You might be lucky. You might
be on the 17.24 from Waterloo
to Charing Cross and happen
to be glancing left precisely when
a gap between two buildings
rumbles past with two hard-hatted
men in it, also a mixer
which has finished mixing, a
crusted wheel-barrow and spades.

This can't be willed of course.
It's pure luck if, as you pass,
it happens one hard-hatted man
is at that moment hosing
clean the other's wellington
boots. Don't miss the care he gives,
the way he stoops and comes
in at an angle and the other
lets him do it, trusts him.

Trains come past any minute here
especially at rush hour, the time
for slowly stopping work. You
might be lucky if you took
the 17.21 or 17.28 and happened
to glance left and see the other,
in a gap of what seems happiness
between before and after,
hosing the first one's boots.

Marianne Morris

Little Song War

Crouching down to compel you in this one,
'I'm calling a spade a spade,' says the pot.
'You're black as a knave,' says the kettle.
In reality, both of them are black
now and both of them used to be white.
Civilians get the gist early on. 'He's a creep.'

On their bellies through thick olive branches they creep
in mysterious allegiance, hair flying into space in this one,
continuing the topical debate of black/white.
'We want reasonable, balanced dialogue,' says the pot.
'It's amazing the way they appease civilians with those black
plush toys, as if admitting greater darkness,' points the kettle.

'There has never been anything more black than that kettle,'
says the pot, bought sweat framing the face, the creep
topless omitted from the. Tank passes in back of a black
and white skirt. White stars liquidized in a black hole in this one.
'Out of my way, you puny little kettle,' says the pot.
They spar over aid-boxes, painted metal tops gleaming white.

'Anyway the dance unit is electrifying,' says a spokesman for the White
Foundation, his face pressed into the ground. Where's the kettle?
The pot sees an opportunity. 'I stand here today as a white pot…'
We don't really know what's going on. The kids creep
harder into their nights of loss. Chairs dashed with glass in this one.
The kettle stares into the mirror, scrubbing at the rings of black.

Brief moment of self-realisation. Will nothing quell the black?
Other than persistent and fraudulent repetition of the word white?
That's not real quelling. A sweaty doll grows his breasts in this one.
'The pot, despite our sanctions, continues with its campaign of black.'

Skulls glitter against velvet pockets as the already-dead creep
breaks humanity's balls. 'You cannot be believed,' says the pot.

'This kettle is completely fucking black,' says the pot,
thinking the microphone is off. YouTube swarms in red and black.
The civilians have long lost interest, deeming each of them a creep.
Meanwhile the avant-garde painters ban the use of white.
The avant-garde poets print books with pages all totally black.
The sun sets on a diseased kind of hope in this one.

Beneath the tomb of public opinion forms the crust of your pie.
Your pie, i.e. a kind of having no allegiance to anything,
whether black, white, this creep or that one, kettle or pot.

Andrew Motion

The Fish in Australia

Where the mountains crumbled
and yellow desert began,
where the sun began to smoulder
in a vault of indigo,
I left the metalled road
and found a perfect circle
of still and silent water
fifty yards by fifty,
with hard treeless banks
un-marked by any prints.

Call it a pool of tears
wept by dogs and kangaroos,
or dead transported men.
I considered it a dewpond
but no dew anywhere
ever fell that swarthy colour,
or seemed so like the lid
of a tunnel piercing through
the planet's fiery heart
to the other side and England.

Providence any how
had made me think ahead
and without a moment's pause
I was parked up on the bank
had my rod and spinner ready,
and was flicking out a cast
to find what rose to me.

Nothing rose of course.
A kookaburra guffawed
a mile off in the bush

and a million years ago;
a snack of tiny flies
sizzled round my lips;
and as the dying sun
sank deeper in its vault
a gang of eucalypts
in tattered party dresses
seemed to shuffle closer
and show their interest
in hearing how my line
whispered on the water
(now uniformly solid
ancient beaten bronze),
how the reel's neat click
made the spinner plonk down,
how the ratchet whirred
as I reeled in slow enough
to conjure up the monster
that surely slept below.

As I reeled in slow enough
then suddenly too slow
and the whirling hooks caught hold
of something obstinate.
Not flesh or fish-mouth though.
Too much dead weight for that.
A stone-age log perhaps.
A mass at any rate
that would not change its mind
and snapped the flimsy line
which flew back in my face
as light as human hair.

If not myself at least
the pond lay peaceful then,
with sun now turned to dust
and a moon-ghost in its place

as much like company
as anything complete.

Why not, I thought,
why not
despite the loss to me
continue standing here
and still cast out my line,
my frail and useless lash,
with no better reason now
than watch the thing lie down
then lift and lie again,
until such time arrives
as the dark that swallowed up
the sky has swallowed me.

Edward O'Dwyer

Just by Chance

This is the place we have been coming to since,
this is the hour, and yet just by chance

that the stars were out that first night, and their light, just by chance,
glittering on the Shannon's lurching surface,

a near-full moon suspended over the centre of Thomond Bridge
just by chance of where we were stood on the quay.

And just by chance it was the most brittle silence
with which we had no words to shatter

did I think to remove my coat and place it over your shoulders,
brushed your neck with my fingers just by chance of how they
  shook.

Then, surely, it was just by chance of the way of the tide
that a pair of swans came floating out from the bridge's far side

towards us, and so I learned that swans mate for life
just by chance you'd read it somewhere once, but couldn't remember
  where.

As though just by chance you said that did it occur to me then
I may never have a better opportunity

to kiss you than there and then, that average Wednesday
Limerick was the most romantic place ever and just by chance.

And so gently turning you round to face me,
just by chance of the arbitrary direction of a convenient wind

your russet hair all blown back and so, just by chance,
the whole of your beautiful face staring back at me,

we kissed our first kiss in that unlikeliest of ways
sometimes things happen so perfectly and yet just by chance.

DE Oprava

The Talk's Small

it was a small talk before
over breakfast she ran off
about if fish liked to sing
or disliked a song
water I hoped
as the child to bottle

who had to count & share with you
on fingers in some dry
like toes future

said no as if that rain
I don't love could never
or hate be sung
the air again

Ruth Padel

Learning to Make an Oud in Nazareth

The first day he cut rosewood for the back,
bent sycamore into ribs and made a belly
    of mahogany. *Let us go early to the vineyards*
    and see if the vines have budded.
The sky was blue over the Jezreel valley
    and the gilt dove shone
above the Church of the Annunciation.
The second day, he carved a camel-bone base
    for the fingerboard.
I sat down under his shadow with delight.

The third day he made a nut of sandalwood,
and a pick-guard of black cherry.
    He damascened a rose of horn
    with arabesques
as lustrous as under-leaves of olive beside the sea.
    I have found him whom my soul loves.
He inlaid the sound-hole with ivory swans,
each pair a valentine of entangled necks,
    and fitted tuning pegs of apricot
to give a good smell when rubbed.

The fourth was a day for cutting
high strings of camel-gut. *His left hand*
    shall be under my head.
    For the lower course, he twisted copper
pale as tarmac under frost.
    He shall lie all night between my breasts.
The fifth day he laid down varnish.
Our couch is green and the beams of our house
    are cedar and pine. Behind the neck
he put a sign to keep off the Evil Eye.

My beloved is a cluster of camphire
in the vineyards of Engedi
    and I watched him whittle an eagle-feather, a plectrum
    to celebrate the angel of improvisation
    who dwells in clefts on the Nazareth ridge
where love waits. And grows, if you give it time.
Set me as a seal upon your heart.
On the sixth day the soldiers came
    for his genetic code.
We have no record of what happened.

I was queuing at the checkpoint to Galilee.
I sought him and found him not.
    He'd have been in his open-air workshop –
    I called but he gave me no answer –
the self-same spot
    where Jesus stood when He came from Capernaum
to teach in synagogue, and townsfolk tried
to throw Him from the rocks. *Until the day break*
    and shadows flee away
I will get me to the mountain of myrrh.

The seventh day we set his wounded hands
around the splinters. *Come with me from Lebanon,*
    my spouse, look from the top
    of Shenir and Hermon, from the lions' dens.
On the eighth there were no more days.
I took a class in carpentry and put away the bridal rug.
We started over
with a child's 'oud bought on eBay.
    He was a virtuoso of the 'oud
and his banner over me was love.

Pascale Petit

Blue-and-Gold Macaw Feather

Just a feather on the aviary floor –
I hold it to the light. Sapphire
one side of the shaft, lapis

on the other, like earth's arc
as it tilts into space.

And the underside, sulphur
as a field of rape, is a palette
where cadmiums roil.

I balance the fallen blade
between thumb and forefinger.

I could paint a world
with this brush, these hues.

Is this how God felt as He drew
His colours across the void?

Sheenagh Pugh

Medals

Pacific Star (India)

He used to swear a fog of spices
came curling over the sea
to grip his throat, a day out of Bombay.

Ashore, he broke all the rules, ate fruit
unwashed, pastries from street stalls,
drank the water, took no harm, loved it all.

One day, reading email from Rajastan,
where his granddaughter is on her travels,
he will smile almost like a young man.

Africa Star (Egypt)

Egypt and he got off on the wrong foot.
Cairo, Alexandria, names of romance
merely curled his lip.

Young as he was, wide-eyed, he saw only
squalor and thievery. Never a good word
nor a fond memory.

Not the land's fault. How could it know
the glum sailor scuffing a stone
along the quay,

so far from home, was wishing himself
happy birthday, turning twenty-one
without ceremony?

Atlantic Star (Norway)

The best part of a day to sail
that long, branching fjord,
and we hardly left

the ship's rail. Molten-silver
waterfalls, the clash of white
where ice met cloud,

sentinel firs
loaded with snow, sea-eagles
skirmishing ahead.

Round every bend
something unmissable. He turned
the photographs, nodding.

"We sailed up there, looking
for the *Tirpitz*, hoping
we wouldn't find her."

Russian Convoys Medal (North Cape)

Mid-afternoon
        no daylight left,

the Arctic Ocean
        a monotone

far below
        the edge of Europe.

Warm rooms cut
        deep in the rock,

café, souvenir shop
        and a plaque burnished

for all the young men
        sick as dogs

who could not come in
        out of the storm.

"Hell of a place
        to spend Christmas"

– though, he'd always add,
        worse for the prey,

the shapely *Scharnhorst*,
        her radar blinded,

pack closing in
        and no way home.

Michael Schmidt

In the Woodcutter's Hut

In the woodcutter's hut the mattresses were stuffed
With beech-leaves and their scent. The drifting snow
Blacked out the window, sealed the door, we breathed
Thanks to the stone chimney. In fact,
It wasn't really cold, we had the cask,
Salt beef, the crate and loaves.
                                        How the hours,
The hours slowed down, the nights, then the week also,
How they slowed
To breathing in the dark, the rise and fall,
And the pulse hardly ticking wrist and temple.

It seemed like days and days, we couldn't count,
We didn't talk in the dark, we didn't touch.
The beech trees told their season rosary,
From spring through autumn, over and over.
                                                        Cut
Before the sap was out of them, they stayed
Alive and in the blackout
We hibernated and were unafraid
Because the beech leaves kept telling their story
And when we dozed they lived again on our boughs,
In the good air we swayed, the beech leaves turning
First red, then green, then copper, and bright birds
Swam among them, perched, whetted their bills on our knuckles.
We were the beech boughs, tree skeletons, the gracious copse.
How long we slept! How they made use of us!
Without those mattresses we wouldn't have survived.
Now we're mast and nut and foliage, their bough, their tree.

Hannah Silva

Hello My Friend

I am contacting you with something urgent,
you have always been a good friend
I need to inform you of the following:
It is important that we remain connected,
it is important we don't avoid the subject.
Please switch on your TV and watch the news.

Nothing happens in the world that isn't in the news,
nothing happens in the news that isn't urgent,
nothing happens until there is an urgent subject
and I would not be contacting you my friend,
if it wasn't for the importance of remaining connected,
if it wasn't that so many are following.

There is perhaps something sinister about following
with such attentiveness the many faces of the news.
Sometimes I wonder if we really need to be connected
to an idea, a chink in history that only now is urgent.
I wonder why I feel the need for a friend
when friendship has become a meaningless subject.

Yet I am asking you to stand alongside me on the subject,
I ask you to confess that we have been following
the instructions of a face we both called a friend
and I ask you to smile with me as we state that the news
of this latest update is a shock and that retraction is urgent
and we celebrate the fact that minds have connected.

There was a time when people became connected
when we connected them, became subject
when we subjected them, their ideas were never urgent
until we believed them. They followed and kept following,
we told our stories and our stories became news.
Keep dancing and you will always have a friend.

I understand the world through faces I call friends,
every day I ensure to remain connected.
There are many sources from which I glean news,
in the space above my thoughts I leave 'no subject'.
There are hundreds of people who are following
my brief statements and their replies are always urgent.

Hello my dear friend there is no subject no winning numbers
I am keeping you connected and I am following you,
I've told you the good news and now await your urgent respond.

A Mo Ina _/ Jar

f I cUd capture a mo
I'd av done it by now, I'd B
hovering, an Austin pwrs kinda
img, ina _/ ful of mist.
That's w@ we cllD it –
d tyms we weren't blind
bac frm d pub stumble
he spoke as f he'd raped me
n d tree's branchs brushd
agenst us 4 a mo. d 2 men s@
cYd by cYd n 1of em replayd
d tyms we couldn't DsciB,
lyN bac on d grass n fallN
N2 it, fallN deep so d oder mn
z, m8 she's yrz. Go gt her.
Go gt her m8. &he did.
Didn't you? As f dat wz it,
dat simpl. u thort, 1day n d
fucha der wl B a _/ jar on a
countA ina rm dat l%ks lk
u n l%ks lk M2 n dat jar wl
contain ll deez moments,
n d mist swirls arnd em,
n we'll sumhw B preserved.

Hideko Sueoka

Owl

For Mr. G. P. and Mr. G. A.

I

Now I work without that sign following
D, prior to F. I follow you,
writing about an owl fascinating
my soul, Mr. G. P., far from haiku.

Did you catch calls of an owl in a park
in Paris sounding again and again?
You did? I, too, pick up this song at dark
singing not-'twhoo' but 'coo hmm' in misty rain.

Did you think of this owl as a symbol
of sharp-sightly wisdom in Paris?
In Shanghai this owl signals sin and ill
and bad luck, on a par with cannabis.

In your world, if an Asian owl should light
on you, would you call it or avoid it?

II

Mr. G. A., your brilliant translation
A VOID migrating, landing on my hand,
I, too, look for 'hoot' in variation,
using lipography just as you did.

With your notation, 'twhoo pht' 'twhoo pfft' 'twhoo pht' 'twhoo pfft' 'twhooo',
Do you hark to hoots of an Asian owl?
With my notation, 'coo hmm' 'coo hmmm' 'coo hmm' 'coo hmmm' 'cooo',
Do you grasp such whoops as fair or foul?

An individual ululation
has multi-marks and plural compound chords
varying on points, skirting all canons
that control thoughts, though producing discords.

'Hmm', 'twhoo pht' 'coo pht' 'twhooo pht' 'cooo pht' 'twhoo
hmm' 'coo hmm' 'twhoo pfft' 'coo pfft'.
How would you hoot owl's fuzzy sound? Just how?

III

Thoughtful old owl, you stand in a brown oak.
You do not talk, you do but mull and gird;
You do but mull and gird, you do not talk;
Not all can do as you do, thoughtful bird.

O awful owl, you scowl in a ginkgo.
You go off, swooping out, and up and down.
And a dark bass doom thrums in your lingo.
How swift is your flight, how grim is your frown!

In soft wind, twhoo by twhoo, 'twhoo pht' 'twhoo pht' 'twhoo
pfft' 'twhoo'
is 'coo hrnm' 'coo hrnm' 'coo hrnmm' 'coo hrnmm' 'cooo hm'
'cooo hm' 'coo' 'coo' 'hoot',
or 'uu ho' 'uuu ho' 'uuuu ho' 'uu ho' 'uuu'.
And your singular cry grows variant.

And although mystical your haunting call,
owl is owl is owl for you – that is all.

*Mr. G. P. is Georges Perec who wrote the novel 'La Disparition'
('A VOID').*
Mr. G. A. is Gilbert Adair who translated the novel into English.

Maggie Sullivan

World Circular

Rumour has it
a rat suspected a goldfish
and told a cat, who threw the rumour to a dog
on a long lead. Dog fetched the rumour back to a
postman, who delivered it to a butcher, baker and candlestick
maker, all right minded citizens. They petitioned the Prime Minister,
who called for more evidence. More evidence followed. The Prime Minister
deemed the rumour irrefutable, telephoned Mr President. Mr President yelled
"fundamental", and wanted to know where the rumour had started, put
everyone under surveillance, even God, even Mrs Smith's canary.
Mr President even had himself put under surveillance. Every
animate and inanimate thing in this universe put under
surveillance, except for the goldfish,
long gone so rumour
has it.

David Tait

Puppets

The puppets are in love
and so are the puppeteers.

You can spot this easily in puppets,
in the clumsy grace with which

one removes his hat, bows
for the happiness of an audience.

The stitched on smile is no less
sincere: he's in love with the rag

of a girl dancing to the music box,
twirling as she does each night,

bead eyes reflecting the light
of love. But look more closely

at the puppeteers, for the true art
lies in them: their hand-gestures,

that look that says:
I'm yours if you'll have me

I'll take off my hat as you dance
to the music box, I'll smile

my stupid stitched on smile
as light reflects your dilated eyes.

Love everywhere, and so much of it;
so much you can hardly see the strings.

Philip Terry

CANTO I

Halfway through a bad trip
I found myself in this stinking car park,
Underground, miles from Amarillo.

Students in thongs stood there,
Eating junk food from skips,
flagmen spewing E's,

Their breath of fetid
Myrrh and ratsbane,
doners

And condemned chicken shin
rose like
distemper.

Then I retched on rising ground;
Rabbits without ears, faces eaten away
by myxomatosis

Crawled towards a bleak lake
to drink
of leucotomy.

The stink would revive a
sparrow, spreadeagled on
a lectern.

It so horrified my heart
I shat
botox.

Here, by the toxic water,
    lay a spotted trout, its glow
    lighting paths for the VC.

And nigh the bins a giant rat,
Seediness oozing from her Flemish pores,
Pushed me backwards, bit by bit

Into Square 5,
        where the wind gnaws
          and sunshine is spent.

By the cashpoint
    a bum asked for a light,
    hoarse from long silence, beaming.

When I saw him gyrate,
His teeth all wasted,
                natch,

His eyes
    long dead
    through speed and booze,

I cried out
          'Take pity,
Whatever you are, man or ghost!'

'Not man, though formerly a man,'
    he says, 'I hail from Providence,
          Rhode Island, a Korean vet.

Once I was a poet, I wrote
          of bean spasms,
        was anthologised in *Fuck You*.'

'You're never Berrigan, that spring
Where all the river of style freezes?'
I ask, awe all over my facials.

'I'm an American
        Primitive,' he says,
'I make up each verse as it comes,

By putting things
                where they
        have to go.'

'O glory of every poet, have a light,
May my Zippo benefit me now,
And all my stripping of your *Sonnets*.

You see this hairy she-rat
                that stalks me like a pimp:
Get her   off my back,

                for every vein and pulse
Throughout my frame she hath
                        made quake.'

'You must needs another way pursue,'
He says, winking while I shade my pin,
'If you wouldst 'scape this beast.

Come, she lets none past her,
Save the VC; if she breathes on you,
                you're teaching nights.

This way, freshman, come,
If I'm not far wrong we can find
A bar, and talk it over with Ed and Tom.'

I went where he led, across a square
And down some steps,
following the crowd.

The SU bar, where we queued
For 30 minutes
To get a watery beer, was packed;

Ed and Tom
Sat at a banquette in the corner
Chain-smoking and swapping jokes.

Here we joined them,
till closing time,
the beer doing the talking.

'Look,' said Tom, 'if this guy's got funding
And approval from the Dean and whatever,
Why not take him round?'

'Show him the works,' said Ed, 'no holds barred!'
'You mean,' said Berrigan, 'give him
a campus tour,

Like, give him Hell?'
'That's exactly what I mean,' said Ed.
'Let's drink to it!' said Tom,

At which we all raised our glasses,
Unsteadily, clinking them together above
The full ashtray.

'Hell,' pronounced Berrigan gnomically,
'Is other people. Sartre said that.
Hell is Hell. I said that.'

Now people were leaving,
we shifted outside,
Into the cold air,

Where we lingered a moment sharing a last
Cigarette, then split,
Ed and Tom going to their digs

Leaving me and Ted to breathe the night air.

Róisín Tierney

Gone

When we're gone from this earth – all of us, I mean –
and our planet shrugs back to her old self again,
carries perhaps a high fever for a while
or shrouds herself in ice and snow;
when our buildings have fallen, our pavements cracked open,
and trees and creepers reclaimed their ground;
when our paintings have long been eaten by mould,
our writings crumbled to zilch;
when even our plastic detritus, the acres in landfill sites
and miles that swirl in the ocean, has rubbed itself to bits;
when our own great star thinks about dying
and making more silver and gold in her heart
as she does so, and spawning baby planets;
after a while, back home in the mud,
maybe a thing with diminishing fins and a backbone
will wriggle out of the slime and look up,
make soft noises that sound a little like 'clucks' to itself –
an early version of us, only better –
and everything will start all over again.

When we're gone, with all of our languages dead,
our prayers and hopes folded to nothing,
where'll be the proof that we ever existed?
Only our TV and radio shows?
Radio waves persist, *ad infinitum*,
keep on travelling onwards, outwards,
which means in two-thousand-four-hundred, approximately,
the Simpsons, comfortable in their yellow skins
and bickering noisily with each other (*D'oh!*),
will begin to enter intergalactic space,
where, perhaps, alien beings
with ears the size of the mind of God
and unimaginably vast intelligence,

will howl with laughter, collapse in the aisles,
or, puzzled, cock their heads to one side.
And when they hear, all those millions of light years away,
a recording of, say, *The Lark Ascending*,
their own hearts, if they have them, will soften and open,
and though they may not know what a metaphor is –
their vast intelligence being strictly literal –
they will, I feel sure of it, weep for joy.

Helen Tookey

Among the Gods (Persephone)

Who is the god, not of gardens but of
their edge-lands? O, give over,
Priapos, we all know about *you*, creeping up

on the lovely Lotis, looking
to give her one to remember you
by, but a couple of brays

from some dumb ass and you've lost the plot
and your hard-on, the nymphette
scarpered. – No, this is a subtler god,

he of the poison-fingers,
digitalis purpurea, spiring the
shady places past the orchard,

pink bells mottled with platelets, some pretty
disease, and each white blotch with
its own pinprick fever-spot. – A better

seducer than you, Priapos,
he knows the lovely lady belladonna,
anemone, crocus, small

and secret wings of cyclamen – and yes,
of course, the orchid. He's the one
who slips the ice-bright seed between my lips

and with it comes the knowledge
I was always, always his.

Rory Waterman

Access Visit

Your afternoon pint; my Britvic pineapple juice;
a bag of prawn cocktail gaping in the middle.
The lounge at the Wig & Mitre was Daddy's choice.
And then, at six, my taxi home; a cuddle
before I left you waving at the corner,
bound for my mother, our monthly weekend over.
And she would always seem a little warmer
than when I'd left, and I'd be slightly colder.

How could I know what an alcoholic was?
The Wig & Mitre's now Widow Cullen's Well.
The snugs have been pulled out, the walls made bare;
but the place still has the same sweet, musty smell,
and I'm going in for a drink again because
I know I'll find a part of us in there.

Stephen Watts

My Grandfather Worked in Pizza Express…

My grandfather worked in Pizza Express in Greek
Street in 1904

Except it wasn't Pizza Express then, it was Crameri
& Caruso's Italian Coffee Parlour

And my grandfather was second-head waiter and my

Mother was not far off being born in Phoenix Street in
the tenements opposite the theatre, the tenements
that were there until the seventies, until that is

They were pulled down & something else was put up
in their place, because it was regeneration time

And there's a photograph of her peeping round from
behind the ice-cream vendor's barrow as
if she knew what was to come

And every Sunday she'd go with her mother & father
to the red church in Soho Square

The church where a piece of cornice fell off & clipped
the biretta of a passing priest, o that priest
will pass by there no more,

And every Thursday for years after they'd moved to
the Creamery out in West Croydon – the one
in the arcade opposite the station

Every Thursday my grandfather'd take his daughter,
my mother, back into Soho to get the gossip,
the fresh pasta & spinach

And they'd sit in Lui Crameri's, he talking dialect with
his cronies, she squashed stiff into a windowless
corner unable to squeak

That same year Stalin & Lenin were over-nighting it
in Tower House in Fieldgate Street over here
for the 3rd International

And the Italian anarchists of Dean St. & Clerkenwell
glistened as they waited under the dewy moon
with greased daggers drawn

Hoping with surety that what would happen could be
swayed and vectored out of sync so that their
century might not have been

What, of course, it had to be. But no : it couldn't, it
couldn't, it simply couldn't be !

My grandfather painted ceilings somewhere in Soho,
bright with mountains in the sunlit snow &
virgin spirits in their peacock shrines !

And I stand here now in Fieldgate Street watching as
a corner of zinc flies from the coppice roof to
land by my unflummoxed feet

And I take the found zinc object as a door-stop for my
hearthless home – we who have to live in some
new degenerate regeneration zone

And as I eat my *fiorentina* in Frith Street I remember
all of this, and all I can say to the waitress who's
asking 'Would I like another coffee yet'

Is 'what is the number of this century we are living in'
& 'how did we get to where duplicity is become
the ordinary nature of our breath ?'

& 'political hurt can hurt us no more' & 'the noise of
the heart is a furtive claw' & 'the remote places
are the heart of our world'

& 'the colours of blood are war-flags unfurled' & 'the
war against terror is an error of fear' & 'all
of us shimmie toward ordinary death'

Then I paid & rushed out penniless into the peacock-
shrieking street, flummoxed to know I'd
met exactly who I'd had to meet.

Simon Williams

Galileo Galilei

'I can see the fortifications of Santa Rosita, Signor Galilei'

Of course you can, you old fool,
you're looking through a telescope.
You could use it to watch the young girls
brush out their hair in La Frezzeria bedrooms
or point it up to see the Tre Cime di Lavardo
far off in the mountains, but far better,
you could, with the right inclination,
see such details of the six bright spheres,
you would be perfectly astonished.

You could see the phases of our sister Venus,
the way Saturn is haloed, Mars cross-hatched,
the swirling eye that stares from Jupiter's head
and even, though I'm still recording,
can't confirm my lenses have detected it,
a new planet, small and far out from the centre,
a watery, icy place, cold as Poseidon.
You could see all this, and if your head
weren't full of banquets and crystal rings,
conclude we're all of us, God willing,
rotating slowly round the Sun.

The first line is spoken by The Doge of Venice in Galileo Galilei *by Bertholt Brecht*

Emily Wills

Still Life with Lobster Pots

It's not how you remember it – scabbed with lichen,
door stuck, boat gone, only lobster pots to mark
where the old man sat finnicking his nets,

fishstink last-gasping in the bucket
you couldn't look at, and gulls scooping
for innards and eyes. The cliff path paused for breath

between that still-living catch and afterwards, that much
is certain. Now the shack retreats into its pelt
of marram and thrift, the tamarisks fray in the wind.

But the lobster pots and nets endure, roped in your mind,
with their orange buoys and easy bait,
so it's impossible to reverse

for even this much remembering has claws,
an awkward tail. The fisherman just goes on being there
with his lapful of holes, his pincer hands mending nothing

but spaces for water to swim through. It's a question
of what escapes, what's trapped for recollection
in this seablue light with its glint and penknife,

its double barb. And probably there are others with you –
forgotten ones, ghosts – for you're not alone in this catch
of random memory, where what remains is cut

to a square of net, a lobster's rearview porthole,
scraps, scales, shells. For the fisherman's knots will hold
and you'll walk on, you and the others, past boatwreck

and lichened rock, as the path curves inland, and looking back
the view will be roped off by tamarisks to a whiff of salt,
a single gull scanning the place for bones.

Mary Woodward

The White Valentine

This year, at last, I could send you a valentine –
a white card in a white envelope, your name
and address stuck on in crooked, cut out letters;
but don't worry, there's no ransom note inside.
I have nothing to bargain with or for, nothing.

Your bewilderment will increase as you pull out
the folded card – empty, unmarked,
off white watercolour paper,
rough edges as if torn by hand, the fold
scored with a bone bookmaker's tool. Almost
a work of art in its blankness and lack.

You'll turn it over, hold it up to the light.
Nothing. You'll look at the envelope again.
Postmarked Central London, though I have considered
going to Paris to post it. Almost any city
would have done: Oslo, Anchorage, Helsinki – somewhere
still deep in snow would have been suitable.
A cold gift, a white valentine from a winter place
heart-high in ice, where they speak another language
and the flights out are grounded.

You might throw it away. Or slip it
in one of your books, think about it now and then.
You will never know who sent it. No point even trying to guess.
I vanished from your life so long ago even the idea of youth
is beyond thaw; your name in my old diary hangs
dangerously in a fragile icicle of memory,
this uncreated card as perfect as everything that didn't happen

Risotto

I'd work from recipes, measure carefully, hover
anxiously. Be so bored by the craft and science
I'd then lose all interest in eating it.
So I cooked risotto every night for a month,
made it instinctive, natural, a simple habit,
as if I'd grown up in a red tiled Italian town
where emerald basil sprouts wildly in the gutters.

Rice, onion, garlic abandoned into hot butter
without a thought. Pepper. Bubbling white wine.
Stock, slipping from a jug uncalculated.
Dared break the cardinal rule never to leave it.
Judged by eye. Knew by the soft heaving gloss
when to let saffron or prawns or asparagus
fall from my heedless hands. Got it so perfect

I can start from scratch, soon be piling plates,
like breathing, like walking, like humming Puccini,
as if another woman, olive eyed, laughing
like Sunday church bells all the while, has done it.

Publisher acknowledgements

Mir Mahfuz Ali · HURRICANE · MIDNIGHT, DHAKA, 25 MARCH 1971 · *Midnight, Dhaka* · Seren

Fiona Benson · DEVONPORT · BREASTFEEDING · *Bright Travellers* · Cape Poetry

Liz Berry · NAILMAKING · BLACK COUNTRY · *Black Country* · Chatto & Windus

Eavan Boland · THE LONG EVENINGS OF THEIR LEAVETAKINGS · *A Woman Without a Country* · Carcanet

Daniel Boon · CRESCENDO · Poetry & Audience

Penny Boxall · WHAT YOU MEAN TO ME · *Ship of the Line* · Eyewear Publishing

Andrea Brady · EXPORT ZONE · *Cut from the Rushes* · Reality Street

Colette Bryce · DERRY · A CLAN GATHERING · *The Whole & Rain-domed Universe* · Picador Poetry

Ian Burnette · DUTCH BABY · Foyle Young Poets of the Year Award

John Burnside · A RIVAL · ON THE VANISHING OF MY SISTER, AGED 3, 1965 · *All One Breath* · Cape Poetry

Niall Campbell · 'THE LETTER ALWAYS ARRIVES AT ITS DESTINATION' · HARVEST · *Moontide* · Bloodaxe Books

Brendan Cleary · IT'S OUR DANCE · *Face* · Pighog

Graham Clifford · THE BEST POEM EVER WRITTEN · *The Hitting Game* · Seren

David Constantine · THE REC · *Elder* · Bloodaxe Books

Robert Crawford · HERAKLEITOS · *Testament* · Cape Poetry

Theodore Deppe · SHOUTING AT THE WINDOWS OF THE NIGHT · *Beautiful Wheel* · Arlen House

Imtiaz Dharker · TALKER · *Over the Moon* · Bloodaxe Books

Douglas Dunn · GUYANE · The Dark Horse

Josh Ekroy · GUIDED TOUR · *Ways to Build a Roadblock* · Nine Arches Press

Carrie Etter · IMAGINED SONS 9: GREEK SALAD · *Imagined Sons* · Seren

John Foggin · CAMERA OBSCURA · Lumen/Camden Poetry Competition

S J Fowler · TREPIDATION · *The Rottweiler's Guide to the Dog Owner* · Eyewear Publishing

Tom French · THE DELIVERY ROOM · *Midnightstown* · The Gallery Press

Beatrice Garland · Beach Holiday · Lady and Fox · *The Invention of Fireworks* · Templar Poetry

Louise Glück · An Adventure · The Horse and Rider · *Faithful and Virtuous Night* · Carcanet

Jen Hadfield · Definitions · *Byssus* · Picador Poetry

David Harsent · Fire: a Song for Mistress Askew · London Review of Books

Lee Harwood · Naming the Names · *The Orchid Boat* · Enitharmon Press

Colin Herd · Rug Design · *Glovebox* · Knives Forks and Spoons

Caoilinn Hughes · Gathering Evidence · *Gathering Evidence* · Carcanet

Alexander Hutchison · Adrift is Maybe Not the Word · Gavia Stellata · *Bones & Breath* · Salt

August Kleinzahler · Epistle xxxix · *The Hotel Oneira* · Faber & Faber

Martin Kratz · The Man Who Walked Through Walls · The Interpreter's House

Hannah Lowe · The Other Family · Kaffeeklatsch

Seán Lysaght · Storm Diary · *Carnival Masks* · The Gallery Press

Lydia Macpherson · Lithium Lovesong · *Love Me Do* · Salt

Lorraine Mariner · Strangers · *There Will Be No More Nonsense* · Picador Poetry

Ian McEwen · Father Lost Lost · *Intermittent Beings* · Cinnamon Press

Kei Miller · Establishing the Metre · In Which the Cartographer Asks for Directions · *The Cartographer Tries to Map a Way to Zion* · Carcanet

Hubert Moore · Hosing Down · McLellan Poetry Prize

Marianne Morris · Little Song War · *The On All Said Things Moratorium* · Enitharmon Press

Andrew Motion · The Fish in Australia · Poem Magazine

Tom Nolan · Red Wing Correctional Facility · Troubadour International Poetry Prize

Edward O'Dwyer · Just by Chance · *The Rain on Cruise's Street* · Salmon Poetry

DE Oprava · The Talk's Small · *The Last Museum of Laughter* · Knives Forks and Spoons

Ruth Padel · Learning to Make an Oud in Nazareth · *Learning to Make an Oud in Nazareth* · Chatto & Windus

Pascale Petit · Blue-and-Gold Macaw Feather · *Fauverie* · Seren

Kevin Powers · GREAT PLAIN · BLUE STAR MOTHER · *Letter Composed During a Lull in the Fighting* · Hodder & Stoughton
Sheenagh Pugh · MEDALS · *Short Days, Long Shadows* · Seren
Vidyan Ravinthiran · SNOW · A CHAIR ADDRESSES JACKIE CHAN · *Grun-tu-molani* · Bloodaxe Books
Denise Riley · AFTER LA ROCHEFOUCAULD · Eggbox/UEA Poetry Series
Stephen Santus · IN A RESTAURANT · Bridport Prize
Michael Schmidt · IN THE WOODCUTTER'S HUT · *The Stories of My Life* · Smith/Doorstop
Hannah Silva · HELLO MY FRIEND · A MO INA _/ JAR · *Forms of Protest* · Penned in the Margins
Hideko Sueoka · OWL · Troubadour International Poetry Prize
Maggie Sullivan · WORLD CIRCULAR · *The Remote* · Waterloo Press
David Tait · PUPPETS · *Self-Portrait with the Happiness* · Smith/Doorstop
Philip Terry · CANTO I · *Dante's Inferno* · Carcanet
Róisín Tierney · GONE · *The Spanish-Italian Border* · Arc Publications
Helen Tookey · AMONG THE GODS (PERSEPHONE) · *Missel-Child* · Carcanet
Jack Underwood · 'THANK YOU FOR YOUR EMAIL' · The White Review
Jeffrey Wainwright · AN EMPTY STREET · PN Review
Rory Waterman · ACCESS VISIT · *Tonight the Summer's Over* · Carcanet
Stephen Watts · MY GRANDFATHER WORKED IN PIZZA EXPRESS... · *Ancient Sunlight* · Enitharmon Press
Hugo Williams · LOVE POEM · I KNEW THE BRIDE · *I Knew the Bride* · Faber & Faber
Simon Williams · GALILEO GALILEI · Fire River Poets Open Poetry Competition
Emily Wills · STILL LIFE WITH LOBSTER POTS · The Frogmore Papers
Mary Woodward · THE WHITE VALENTINE · RISOTTO · *The White Valentine* · Worple Press

Biographies of the shortlisted writers

Forward Prize for Best Collection

COLETTE BRYCE (b. 1970 Derry) spent much of her twenties reading contemporary poetry while working as a bookseller in London. She started to write poems in the early 1990s. After publishing her first collection in 2000, Bryce won a literary fellowship and has worked freelance as a writer and editor ever since. *The Whole & Rain-domed Universe*, her fourth collection, centres on her Derry childhood and questions the nature of memory and the emigrant's perspective. Bryce was awarded first prize in the National Poetry Competition and the Cholmondeley Award from the Society of Authors in 2010. She cites Emily Dickinson, Louis MacNeice and Karen Solie as inspirations.

Her advice to would-be poets: 'Enjoy the journey. Read widely. Write the poems that only you can write.'

JOHN BURNSIDE (b. 1955 Dunfermline) describes his Catholic childhood in Corby as solitary: 'Reading poetry was probably the only real education I had in anything.' Poetry, he says, is 'a defence of care over the language, its richness, its subtleties, its possibilities'. He believes that 'if we keep reading poetry, and so educating ourselves in metaphor, we can see through and scoff at the deceptive myths peddled by certain politicians and salespeople.'

He became a writer while working as a software engineer. His novels, memoirs and poems have won many awards and his 2011 collection *Black Cat Bone* won both the Forward Prize and the TS Eliot Prize.

All One Breath, his thirteenth poetry collection, was inspired by Ecclesiastes: 'For that which befalleth the sons of men befalleth beasts… yea, they have all one breath.' Our kinship with all living things is a matter, he maintains, for awe.

His advice to would-be poets: 'Do it for love. Listen to music. Read the classics, read your contemporaries, get advice from other readers, read in translation. Read, read, read.'

LOUISE GLÜCK (b. 1943 New York City), has written poetry for as long as she can remember. She was US Poet Laureate from 2003-4 and has won the Pulitzer Prize, the National Book Critics Circle Award and the William Carlos Williams Award. As a child with 'a premature sense of vocation', she was inspired by Blake's *Songs of Innocence* and songs from Shakespeare's plays. As a teenager, she sent off manuscripts to publishers. 'It was good practice,' she says, 'that decade of rejection.'

Faithful and Virtuous Night took five years to write: when stuck, she would turn to the very short stories of Kafka for inspiration. She finds DH Lawrence's 'great, imperfect poems' encouraging and draws from the work of younger poets and her own students.

Her advice to would-be poets: 'Persist. Stay, or become, capable of change. Trust what seems an adventure however confusing.'

KEI MILLER (b. 1978 Kingston, Jamaica) enrolled in Creative Writing Poetry at the University of the West Indies because the Fiction course he wanted to take was full. 'I thought of poetry as just an exercise that would make me write better fiction but it took over,' he says.

In his first short story collection, *The Fear of Stones and Other Stories*, he wrote of homophobia in Jamaica. It was shortlisted in 2007 for the Commonwealth Writers' Best First Book prize. He has a PhD in Caribbean Literature from the University of Glasgow, where, until recently, he taught creative writing.

The Cartographer Tries to Map a Way to Zion, his third poetry collection, was prompted by his realisation that 'maps pretend to be innocent, but aren't'. He finds parallels between the rules governing the reckoning of distance, size and location and the rules imposed by poetic form. Quoting the poet Kamau Brathwaite, he observes 'the hurricane does not roar in pentameters'.

His advice to would-be poets: 'Allow your work to be shaped by voices that aren't poetic voices, people who have never thought of themselves as poets.'

HUGO WILLIAMS (b. 1942 Windsor) first wrote poetry aged 13, copying Laurie Lee and the Movement poets. 'I liked writing,' he says, 'because I could do it and it cheered me up.' Recently, while enduring the dialysis treatment that forms the subject of some of the poetry in *I Knew the Bride*, he has attempted more abstract styles and virtually 'nonsense' poems: 'I see these as my future because my mind is going.'

Poetry, for Williams, is an opportunity to say the unsayable, 'a search for meaning rather than an extension of existing thoughts'. He cites Michael Hofmann, Ian Hamilton and Philip Larkin as inspirations.

His advice to would-be poets: 'Don't have anything to do with universities or creative writing courses.'

Forward Prize for Best First Collection

FIONA BENSON (b. 1978 Wroughton) began keeping a poetry notebook at 17 on hearing that someone she knew wrote poetry. Suddenly, poetry 'seemed permissible and possible'. She discovered Seamus Heaney, Sylvia Plath and Emily Dickinson at this time. Although she considered becoming an actor or a lawyer, she says 'poetry just gradually became the thing I depended on'. *Bright Travellers* is arranged in sequences on miscarriage, childbirth and motherhood, interspersed with stand-alone bridging poems. One sequence, 'Love-Letter to Vincent', is inspired by Van Gogh and is written in the voice of his prostitute mistress. Benson says there is 'a certain amount of slippage between this voice and my more usual lyric I'. In 2006 Benson won an Eric Gregory Award and a Faber New Poets Award.

LIZ BERRY (b. 1980 Black Country) says that poetry 'was really a secret love' until her mid-twenties. While working as an infant school teacher, she took night classes in poetry before studying in 2008 for an MA at Royal Holloway with Jo Shapcott and Andrew Motion. 'Everything came alive for me that year,' Berry says, 'and I began reading and writing with a fury.' In 2009, she received an Eric Gregory Award and in 2012, she was selected for the Jerwood/Arvon Mentoring Scheme and was mentored by Daljit Nagra. He encouraged Berry to use the dialect of her friends and family in her writing. 'I wanted to tell a story about the place where I grew up,' Berry says. 'In many ways, the book (*Black Country*) is a love letter to the Black Country.' Berry draws inspiration from the use of dialect by other poets, including Katrina Porteous and Billy Letford.

NIALL CAMPBELL (b. 1984 South Uist) began writing poetry as an undergraduate at the University of Glasgow. 'Reading poetry has the almost inevitable effect of encouraging one to write,' Campbell explains, 'because by reading poetry you find yourself enjoined in a conversation between the poet and those gone before and those that might come after.' He has tried to achieve a unity of tone, image and atmosphere in *Moontide*. He describes his tastes as 'Celtic', naming Seamus Heaney, Don Paterson, John Glenday and Kathleen Jamie as inspirations. In 2011, Campbell received an Eric Gregory Award, followed by a Jerwood/Arvon mentorship in 2013.

Beatrice Garland (b. 1938 Oxford) describes writing as 'a marvellous part of one's interior private life' and cites John Donne, John Clare and Seamus Heaney as inspirations. At school, she was punished for misdemeanours by being forced to memorise poetry. 'Whole lines and particular individual words themselves became, like sweets, something that could be saved up and enjoyed for their marvellous taste,' Garland explains. In 2001, she won the National Poetry Prize. She wrote no poetry for a while afterwards, but focused on her work as an NHS clinician and researcher in psychological medicine. She won the Strokestown International Poetry Competition in 2002 and was shortlisted for the inaugural Picador Poetry Prize. *The Invention of Fireworks* contains about 50 of the 'several hundred' poems Garland has scattered all over the room where she writes.

Kevin Powers (b. 1980 Virginia) fought in Iraq as a machine gunner between 2004 and 2005. He began writing poetry aged 12 after buying a collection by Dylan Thomas in a second-hand book shop. 'I think I wrote my first poem as soon as I finished reading "Fern Hill",' he says. His novel about Iraq, *The Yellow Birds*, won the Guardian First Book Award and is being made into a film starring Benedict Cumberbatch. Powers is a Michener Fellow in poetry at the University of Austin, Texas and cites Larry Levis, Yusef Komunyakaa, Brigit Pegeen Kelly and Dean Young as inspirations for his work, as each 'share a kind of clarity in the face of difficulty and complexity'. *Letter Composed During a Lull in the Fighting* was written after his return from service in Iraq. 'I hoped poetry would allow me to reckon with the difficult questions I had about my service,' Powers says, 'in the same way that I had used it to address all the confusion the world had presented me with since I was a teenager.'

Vidyan Ravinthiran (b. 1984 Leeds) was encouraged by his Sri Lankan parents to consider literature 'a wonderful thing'. He began writing poetry by creating versions of Keats' odes. This changed when he was given the 2002 *Forward Book of Poetry* by a friend of his mother. 'I had these old-fashioned ideas about what a poem should be,' Ravinthiran explains, 'and I couldn't square them with the excitements of free verse.' In 2008, his pamphlet *At Home or Nowhere* was published by tall-lighthouse. He cites Yeats, Philip Larkin and Arun Kolatkar as early inspirations; Elizabeth Bishop is the subject of his doctoral thesis at Cambridge. Ravinthiran describes his collection, *Grun-tu-molani*, as 'the equivalent of the Ravinthiran family Christmas. We have a roast, potatoes, stuffing, gravy, veg, but also a thousand curries… Everything you could want.'

Forward Prize for Best Single Poem

Tim Nolan (b. 1954 Minneapolis) wrote his first poem on the Vietnam War, at the age of 14. 'It was terrible,' he says. 'The poem and the war.' He has since published two collections. The poem included here is one of several written during a one-month residency at the Anderson Center in Red Wing, Minnesota in October 2013, during which he ran a poetry workshop at Red Wing's juvenile detention centre. Garrison Keillor has read a number of Nolan's poems on *The Writer's Almanac* on National Public Radio and others have been published in *The Nation*, *The New Republic* and *Ploughshares*. He cites Shakespeare, Walt Whitman, Emily Dickinson and William Carlos Williams as inspirations, and values poems that have 'serious intentions, but a light touch'.

Denise Riley (b. 1948 Carlisle) uses poetry as 'a way of thinking aloud in a way which is open; not intrusively autobiographical but undefended'. Her work resists the idea of the 'I' in the poem and the author being conflated; she is interested in how the illusion of access to the speaker's poetic soul is created. As a respected feminist philosopher, she has engaged with the issues of identity, motherhood and employment policies for women in post-war Britain. She admires the Elizabethans, Jacobeans and William Blake. She has been Professor of Literature and

Philosophy at the University of East Anglia, a Writer in Residence at the Tate Gallery, London, and has raised three children. The death of her adult son in 2008 prompted 'A Part Song', which won the 2012 Forward Prize for Best Single Poem.

STEPHEN SANTUS (b. 1948 Wigan) has been writing poetry since 1965. His interest was sparked by his older brother who loved to read poetry and Shakespeare aloud. Santus appreciates classical Chinese poets and the Japanese haiku and tanka writers for their delicacy and emotional accessibility. He teaches English in a language school in Oxford, having previously taught in France and Austria. He also admires Philip Larkin and his 'ability to sneak deep truths past you when you think you are just having a pint and a chat at the bar'.

JACK UNDERWOOD (b. 1984 Norwich) is currently studying towards a PhD in Creative Writing at Goldsmiths College, where he also teaches English Literature. His first poem was about a pair of Adidas Gazelle trainers covered in biro graffiti. Underwood enjoyed poetry at school, though he felt that poems were by 'dead people'. After studying Simon Armitage at college, the idea of writing a 'real, live poem' suddenly seemed 'plausible'. His favourite poets include Sam Riviere, Emily Berry – both winners of the Forward Prize for Best First Collection – Jennifer Knox and Philip Larkin. Underwood was included in the Faber New Poets series and co-edits the anthology series *Stop Sharpening Your Knives*.

JEFFREY WAINWRIGHT (b. 1944 Stoke-on-Trent) discovered his love for poetry at school thanks to his English teacher, Ken Lowe. He has long been fascinated by American poetry, from Whitman to Stevens, partly 'because it is not English'. He is drawn, in his writing, to Italian art: 'An Empty Street' was inspired by Ottone Rosai's painting *Via San Leonardo*. While at university in Leeds, Wainwright met and learned from many poets working in or around the English School, including Geoffrey Hill. His first poems published nationally were edited from Leeds by Jon Silkin and Ken Smith. He was editor of *Poetry and Audience*, one of the longest-running poetry magazines in the UK, which celebrated its 60th anniversary last year.

Previous winners of the Forward Prizes

Best Collection

2013 Michael Symmons Roberts *Drysalter* (Jonathan Cape)
2012 Jorie Graham *PLACE* (Carcanet)
2011 John Burnside *Black Cat Bone* (Jonathan Cape)
2010 Seamus Heaney *Human Chain* (Faber and Faber)
2009 Don Paterson *Rain* (Faber and Faber)
2008 Mick Imlah *The Lost Leader* (Faber and Faber)
2007 Sean O'Brien *The Drowned Book* (Picador)
2006 Robin Robertson *Swithering* (Jonathan Cape)
2005 David Harsent *Legion* (Faber and Faber)
2004 Kathleen Jamie *The Tree House* (Picador)
2003 Ciaran Carson *Breaking News* (Gallery Press)
2002 Peter Porter *Max is Missing* (Picador)
2001 Sean O'Brien *Downriver* (Picador)
2000 Michael Donaghy *Conjure* (Picador)
1999 Jo Shapcott *My Life Asleep* (OUP)
1998 Ted Hughes *Birthday Letters* (Faber and Faber)
1997 Jamie McKendrick *The Marble Fly* (OUP)
1996 John Fuller *Stones and Fires* (Chatto)
1995 Sean O'Brien *Ghost Train* (OUP)
1994 Alan Jenkins *Harm* (Chatto)
1993 Carol Ann Duffy *Mean Time* (Anvil Press)
1992 Thom Gunn *The Man with Night Sweats* (Faber and Faber)

Best First Collection

2013 Emily Berry *Dear Boy* (Faber and Faber)
2012 Sam Riviere *81 Austerities* (Faber and Faber)
2011 Rachael Boast *Sidereal* (Picador)
2010 Hilary Menos *Berg* (Seren)
2009 Emma Jones *The Striped World* (Faber and Faber)
2008 Kathryn Simmons *Sunday at the Skin Launderette* (Seren)
2007 Daljit Nagra *Look We Have Coming to Dover* (Faber and Faber)
2006 Tishani Doshi *Countries of the Body* (Aark Arts)
2005 Helen Farish *Intimates* (Jonathan Cape)
2004 Leontia Flynn *These Days* (Jonathan Cape)

2003 AB Jackson *Fire Stations* (Anvil Press)
2002 Tom French *Touching the Bones* (Gallery Press)
2001 John Stammers *Panoramic Lounge-bar* (Picador)
2000 Andrew Waterhouse *In* (The Rialto)
1999 Nick Drake *The Man in the White Suit* (Bloodaxe)
1998 Paul Farley *The Boy from the Chemist is Here to See You* (Picador)
1997 Robin Robertson *A Painted Field* (Picador)
1996 Kate Clanchy *Slattern* (Chatto)
1995 Jane Duran *Breathe Now, Breathe* (Enitharmon)
1994 Kwame Dawes *Progeny of Air* (Peepal Tree)
1993 Don Paterson *Nil Nil* (Faber and Faber)
1992 Simon Armitage *Kid* (Faber and Faber)

Best Single Poem

2013 Nick MacKinnon 'The Metric System' (The Warwick Review)
2012 Denise Riley 'A Part Song' (London Review of Books)
2011 RF Langley 'To A Nightingale' (London Review of Books)
2010 Julia Copus 'An Easy Passage' (Magma)
2009 Robin Robertson 'At Roane Head' (London Review of Books)
2008 Don Paterson 'Love Poem for Natalie "Tusja" Beridze' (Poetry Review)
2007 Alice Oswald 'Dunt' (Poetry London)
2006 Sean O'Brien 'Fantasia on a Theme of James Wright' (Poetry Review)
2005 Paul Farley 'Liverpool Disappears for a Billionth of a Second' (The North)
2004 Daljit Nagra 'Look We Have Coming to Dover' (Poetry Review)
2003 Robert Minhinnick 'The Fox in the Museum of Wales' (Poetry London)
2002 Medbh McGuckian 'She is in the Past, She Has This Grace' (The Shop)
2001 Ian Duhig 'The Lammas Hireling' (National Poetry Competition)
2000 Tessa Biddington 'The Death of Descartes' (The Bridport Prize)
1999 Robert Minhinnick 'Twenty-five Laments for Iraq' (PN Review)
1998 Sheenagh Pugh 'Envying Owen Beattie' (New Welsh Review)
1997 Lavinia Greenlaw 'A World Where News Travelled Slowly' (Times Literary Supplement)